101

PLANS TO PAY LESS TAXES by

The J. K. Lasser Tax Institute

Bernard Greisman, Editor

REVISED EDITION

Published by
Simon and Schuster · New York

Designed by Irving Perkins Associates

Manufactured in the United States of America

10 9 8 7 6 5 4 3 2 1

Library of Congress Cataloging in Publication Data

ISBN: 0–671–52914–5

PREFACE

101 Plans to Pay Less Taxes is a collection of year-round, income-tax-reducing plans for your personal, investment, and business activities.

The plans and techniques range from simple family tax-planning moves to more complex business and investment tax strategies. Here you will find current advice on such topics as making tax shelter investments in real estate and oil and gas ventures, splitting income with your family, using trusts, deciding the best way to deduct business travel expenses, planning exchanges of real estate and other investment property, making year-end moves to reduce taxes, investing for capital gain and tax-exempt income, making tax-wise donations to favorite philanthropies, planning sales of your residence, evaluating business tax options, and avoiding tax penalties.

Our objective is to inform and to provide solutions. At the same time, we have also flagged problem areas which may require the advice of an experienced tax practitioner.

We gratefully acknowledge the contribution of Elliott Eiss, member of the New York Bar, with the assistance of Katherine Torak in the preparation of this book.

Bernard Greisman,
Editor, J. K. Lasser Tax Institute

CONTENTS

9

SHIFT INCOME TO LOWER-BRACKET FAMILY MEMBERS

To reduce the overall tax burden on a family, consider gifts of income-producing property to dependents.

Each additional dollar of ordinary income you receive, such as interest, dividends, and rent, is taxed in your highest bracket. If you can deflect part of this income to your children or other dependent relatives who are in lower tax brackets, they will pay a smaller tax on the income than you will pay. This tax-saving technique is known as income splitting, and allows more after-tax income to remain within the family.

For example, you have investment income of $30,000 which is subject to the top tax rate of 50%. You net $15,000 after taxes. Assume that you can split this income among your three children, and that their income is subject to a tax rate of 15%. Your family will net $25,500; income splitting has saved $10,500.

To split income, you must do more than make gifts of income. You must transfer the property which produces the income. You do not avoid tax on interest by instructing your savings bank to credit interest to your children's accounts. Unless you actually transfer ownership of the account to your children, the interest is earned on your money and must be reported by you. The same holds true with dividends, rental income, and other forms of income. Unless you transfer the property providing the income, the income will be taxed to you.

You may not split earned income; income resulting from your services is taxed to you. Nor may you avoid this result by setting up trusts to receive your earned income. You also may not effectively split income by making interest-free or low-interest loans to a relative who uses the loan for investment purposes. Under a new tax law, you may be subject to gift and income taxes. Income may be imputed using an adjustable interest rate tied to Treasury obligations if the loan exceeds $10,000 or the loan is used to buy or carry investments.

Shifting income-producing property to relatives may generally be accomplished tax free if you stay within certain guidelines. You may give tax free up to $10,000 to each donee each year; further, if your spouse joins in the gift, you may give up to $20,000 tax free to each donee. Thus if you (with your spouse's consent) make gifts to four persons, you could give away up to $80,000 (4 × $20,000 exclusion) without paying gift tax. Gifts exceeding this exclusion are subject to tax. However, a tax credit may eliminate gift tax liability.

Despite the tax advantages, you must decide whether you can afford to give away your property. Predict your future needs as accurately as possible. Further, you must evaluate the ability of your recipients to manage the property you give them. Gifts in trust may be used if your recipient is too young or is unable to manage the property.

USE TRUSTS TO SPLIT FAMILY INCOME

A trust is generally treated as a separate taxpayer. Therefore it may be used as an income-splitting device.

By setting up a number of trusts, a person in a high tax bracket spreads his income among several taxpayers who pay tax at lower rates. The overall result will generally be a smaller tax on the total income earned by him and the trusts than would be payable if he had retained the property and made gifts of after-tax income. A husband or wife who sets up a trust for the benefit of the other will generally remain taxable on trust income that may be used for his or her benefit.

During your lifetime, you may create a trust known as an *inter vivos* trust. In your will, you may authorize the creation of a trust after your death; such a trust is called a testamentary trust. Under both types of trusts, property is transferred to a trustee; an individual, bank or trust company, or a combination may act as trustees. The trustee holds and manages the property for beneficiaries named by you.

An *inter vivos* trust may be irrevocable or revocable. An irrevocable trust requires a complete surrender of property. By conveying property irrevocably to a trust, you relieve yourself from tax on the income from the trust principal. Further, the property in trust usually is not subject to estate tax, although it may be subject to a gift tax.

A trust should be made irrevocable only if you are certain you will not need the trust property in a financial emergency.

In a revocable trust, you reserve the right to revoke the trust. As such, it is considered an incomplete gift and offers no present income tax savings. However, it minimizes any delay in passing property to beneficiaries if you die while the trust is in force.

Short-term trusts. These are widely used for splitting income among family members. Although they are considered irrevocable trusts, you do not have to relinquish ownership rights completely. Generally, as long as the trust period is for at least ten years and a day, income of the trust is taxable to the beneficiaries, not to you. At the end of the trust period, the property may return to you. For example, you can create a trust to pay income to your father as beneficiary. The trust is to exist as long as he lives. At his death the property returns to you. The trust income is not taxed to you, even if your parent's life expectancy is less than ten years. The use of short-term trusts to provide for your children's college education is discussed in another plan.

The transfer of the income interest is subject to gift tax. Current Treasury tables have increased the taxable value of the income interest. The tables assume a 10% rate of return and use the same mortality rate for both men and women. Prior tables used a 6% rate and assumed a lower female mortality rate. For example, under the prior tables, if you created a 10-year trust, you could transfer up to $22,644 without exceeding the $10,000 gift tax exclusion or up to $45,288 if your spouse consents to the gift. Under the new tables, only transfers up to $16,274 come within the exclusion. If your spouse consents to the gift, you may contribute up to $32,548 to come within the exclusion.

Spousal remainder trust. To avoid or reduce gift tax consequences, trust planners suggest the use of a spousal remainder trust, which allows a trust term of less than 10 years. Under the law, the income interest may be less than 10 years because the trust property does not return to you.

The spousal remainder trust pays trust income to a beneficiary for several years, such as your child, and at the end of that income period the trust property passes to your spouse.

The shorter trust term lets you make larger contributions to the trust within the gift tax exclusion than are possible with a 10-year short-term trust. Under the Treasury 10% tables, if you fund a five-year spousal remainder trust by making annual contributions over the five-year period, it is possible to contribute up to $360,000 without gift tax consequences.

You are not taxed on trust income because you have not retained an interest in the trust. However, you may be subject to tax if the trust income pays support expenses of your children. The issue of support for trust funding of college education is discussed in the next plan.

A spousal remainder trust is helpful in meeting the income

needs of a period of less than 10 years. For example, you may want to set up a trust to fund only your child's college education for a four- or five-year period. You may set up a spousal remainder trust for that period.

The spousal remainder trust should not be considered if you anticipate marital difficulties with your spouse.

Accumulation trusts. You may want to direct your trustee to accumulate income for a certain period instead of distributing it as earned. Although the beneficiary will not have to report the income earned by the trust until the year the accumulated amount is received, tax on this amount will be computed as if the accumulations were received in the year they were earned. The law sets out the method for computing the tax on this basis.

An accumulation trust may also produce tax savings by deferring tax payments on income for the beneficiary whose tax bracket is higher than that of the trust.

Trust property. You may transfer almost any kind of income-producing property, such as securities and real estate, to a trust. You may use your stock in a closely held or solely owned corporation. You can place a part of your corporate stock in trust for your child and even make yourself trustee. The dividends and other income earned by these shares will not be taxed to you even though after giving up a minority stock interest to the trust, you still control the corporation.

You may not avoid tax by transferring to a trust payments owed to you. For example, some customers have not yet paid you for your services. You transfer their accounts to a trust set up for your children. Even though the trust later collects on the accounts, the IRS says that you are taxed, not the trust.

You would not want to transfer appreciated property to a trust if you can anticipate that it would be sold within two years. Under general trust rules, the trust is a separate entity which pays tax at its own marginal rate. However, if it sells appreciated property within two years after receiving it from the grantor, the appreciation attributed to the time the grantor held the property will be taxed at the marginal rates of the grantor (including any alternative minimum tax that may be due). Appreciation recognized after the transfer is taxed at the trust's regular rates. The effect of this rule is to tax the property as if the grantor had sold it, paid tax, and then transferred the net proceeds to the trust.

3

SET UP A TRUST TO PROVIDE FUNDS FOR COLLEGE EDUCATION

You may set up a trust to provide funds for your child's college education. Make sure that you will not be taxed on income used by the trust to pay for educational expenses.

Under the tax law, if your legal obligation to support your child is discharged by income from a trust you set up, you are taxed on that income. Whether you are legally obligated to send your child to college is determined by the law of the state in which you live. The current trend of law recognizes that a parent who is financially able to provide a college education for his children has an obligation to do so. This, however, does not mean that the law in your state has reached this conclusion. Review this point with your attorney.

The issue of whether you are obligated to send your child to college might be avoided by setting up the trust when your child is young, say, seven or under. You transfer property to a trust which is to continue until the child reaches college age—a period of at least ten years. You also set up a bank account in the child's name to which trust income is paid, or invest the income in government bonds in the child's name. Before the child reaches college age, the trust ends and you receive the trust property. When your child starts college, he or she begins to withdraw funds from the bank account or to cash in the bonds to pay college expenses. As the trust no longer exists, it has not been used to pay the college costs directly. However, this approach may not be necessary if, in your state, your child reaches legal majority at 18 and is considered an emancipated adult whom you are not obligated to support. Under these circumstances, trust payments of college costs would not be considered a discharge of support obligation.

In setting up the trust, see that the trust deed does not state that income is for educational purposes if there is a danger that you may be held legally obligated to provide a college education. Especially avoid the mistake which one father made: In his negotiations with colleges, he obligated himself to pay his children's college expenses. When the trusts paid these bills, the IRS contended that they were paying expenses the father had legally assumed. A court agreed that when the trust paid the college bills, it was in effect discharging the father's legal obligation; he was taxed on the trust income. Thus a parent may be taxed on trust income on either the support theory or the legal obligation theory. In another case, parents were not obligated under state law (Illinois) to pay the college costs for children over 18 but were held taxable on a payment made by an educational-benefits trust established by their employer for the benefit of their children. Although by law they did not have a legal obligation to educate their children, they testified in court that they felt a parental obligation to do so. The children were also claimed as dependents, indicating that the parents continued to support them. Finally, to argue that the benefits should not be taxable because there is no legal obligation to give the children a college education ignores the realities of parental relationships in our time.

4

TRUST LEASEBACK OF RENTAL PROPERTY

Family income splitting has been successfully executed by professionals and business owners through trust leasebacks of facilities used in their practice or business.

Consider transferring to a trust rental property used in your business or profession and then leasing back the property. This technique allows you to use the premises, claim a rent deduction for its use, and shift income from your higher tax bracket to the lower tax bracket of the trust. Income shifting occurs when rent payments claimed as deductions on your personal return are reported by the trust as rental income which ultimately benefits your children or other dependents who are named trust beneficiaries.

The IRS may attempt to disallow the rent deduction as it has in a number of cases which have been litigated in the courts. However, it has not been successful in cases where there has been an independent trustee, the rent is reasonable, and the lease has a business purpose. The business purpose test is satisfied when your use of the property is essential to your business or profession. Also helpful in securing the deduction may be evidence that there are other tenants in the building and that the trust term exceeds ten years.

After the trust term, you may recover the property. However, in such a case the IRS may argue that this reversionary interest gives you an equity interest in the property which bars you from deducting the rent. The Tax Court, however, holds that the retention of a reversionary interest is not an equity which affects the right to deduct rent. Deductions of rent have been denied when the transfer fails to shift any real control to an independent trustee, or the grantor names himself or herself as trustee and retains substantially the same control over the property as before transferring the property to the trust.

Be aware when setting up a trust of mortgaged property that if you are personally liable on the mortgage, you are taxed when the trust pays off any of the interest or principal.

SPLIT BUSINESS INCOME WITH YOUR FAMILY

Tax on your business income may be reduced if you can shift some of it to members of your family. You may also avoid estate tax on the value of the capital interests transferred to children.

Business income may be shifted by forming a family partnership or by transferring stock to a family member. If the gift of a business interest does not exceed the annual gift tax exclusion of $10,000 for each recipient ($20,000 on gifts made by a husband and wife), the transfer is not subject to gift tax.

In a partnership, a minor child will be recognized as a partner if he or she is competent to manage property or the minor's interest is placed in trust for his or her benefit.

In the case of a family corporation, stock may be transferred to a trust or to a custodian account in which the parent may act as custodian. There is less red tape in setting up a custodian account. However, a transfer will not be effective if the parents in fact continue to operate the business as before, ignoring the transfer of the stock to the minor. For example, in one case two owners of a beer distributorship operating as an S corporation gave all of their stock to their children. Their objective was to shift income to the children. The plan failed because the fathers continued to run the corporation as if the stock transfers had not been made. As key employees and directors of the corporation, they retained complete control over the business. The children exercised no voice in corporate affairs. No custodian or guardian was appointed to represent the minor children's interests as stockholders. Further, despite substantial company profits, the children received only a small amount as dividends, generally enough only to offset the inclusion of corporate income on their returns. On the other hand, the fathers continued to take sizable unsecured interest-free loans from the corporation, as they had before the stock transfer.

If stock in an S corporation is transferred to a trust, the trust must meet certain tests in order to safeguard the S election.

Shifting income is more difficult in a service business. For example in a service partnership, a gift of a partnership interest to a family member will not shift partnership income unless the relative actually performs services for the partnership. Similarly in an S corporation, pass through items must reflect the value of services rendered or capital contributed by family members of the shareholders. If a relative of an S corporation shareholder performs services for the corporation or loans money to the corporation without receiving reasonable pay or interest, the IRS may allocate income to reflect the value of the services or capital provided. The term "family" of an individual includes only spouse, ancestors, lineal descendants, and any trusts for the primary benefit of such persons.

HOW TO CHOOSE PROPERTY FOR GIFTS

You may want to give real estate or securities as gifts. There are generally no income tax consequences to making a gift unless the property is subject to debt that exceeds your cost basis. However, project tax consequences when choosing what property to give.

If you want to make a gift of property, compare your basis with its current value. If the value of the property has dropped below your cost, it is not advisable to give it away. If the donee sells it, he or she may not deduct the loss based on the drop in value. The basis for tax purposes becomes the market value at the time of the gift. The loss deduction is lost forever—for you or anyone else. It may be preferable to sell the property, make a gift of the proceeds, and deduct the tax loss.

If the property has appreciated in value and you give it away, the donee will realize a gain in selling the property. If he or she is in a lower income tax bracket than you are, a sale of the property will be at a lower tax than if you sold it. If this tax saving exceeds any gift tax cost to you, then this appreciated property might be given without adverse tax cost. On the other hand it may be advisable to hold property which has substantially appreciated in value so that it will be included in your estate. Since your heir will get a stepped-up basis, the appreciation will escape income tax. Compare your heir's income tax saving because of the stepped-up basis with the tax, if any, your estate would pay on the asset.

If the property produces income which you do not need, a transfer of the property to a family member or trust in a lower tax bracket than yours will produce tax savings.

It is generally inadvisable to give away property if there are outstanding mortgages or other debts exceeding your basis in the property because the IRS will require you to recognize the excess of debt over basis as gain subject to tax. Take this case:

Levine transferred a building he had owned for 19 years to a trust for his grandchildren. Over the years he had obtained $672,000 in nonrecourse loans on the property, in addition to a $108,000 mortgage outstanding when he obtained the property; $127,000 of the loans was repaid and $334,000 of the loan proceeds was invested in the building in the form of improvements. The trust took the building subject to all outstanding loans on it. At the time of transfer the mortgages and other liabilities exceeded Levine's basis by $425,000. The IRS charged that this excess was taxable gain to Levine. Levine argued that no gain is recognized on the making of a gift, that any potential gain is preserved in the basis, and that the donee eventually reports gain when he sells the property. The Tax Court and an appeals court sided with the IRS. The transfer was part sale, part gift. Levine received a tangible economic benefit measured by the excess of mortgages and other liabilities over his adjusted basis.

MAKE GIFTS TO MINORS USING CUSTODIAN ACCOUNTS

A custodian account is an inexpensive, simple way to make gifts to minors while retaining control until the child is age 18 or 21.

You can provide for the college education of a minor by making a gift of stocks paying dividends or bonds paying interest to a custodian account, naming yourself or another relative as custodian. You remain custodian until the minor is legally considered an adult. You simply transfer securities to a custodian account for the benefit of a minor. There is no need for a legal guardianship or a trust. Although custodian accounts may be opened anywhere in the United States, the legal rules governing them may vary from state to state. The differences in the state laws generally do not affect federal tax consequences.

For income tax purposes, the minor pays the tax on income derived from the securities held in the account. However, if that income is used to support or maintain the minor, it is taxable to the person who has the legal duty to support him.

For example, you are in the 50% income tax bracket, are married, and have one child, John, age six. You live in New York where the Uniform Gift to Minors Act is part of the Personal Property Law. You purchase $6,000 worth of income-producing securities and have them registered in your name "as custodian, for John Jones, a minor, under Article 8-A of the Personal Property Law of New York."

This investment produces $600 of income a year which you accumulate as if it were a trust. You do not use any of this income for the support of your son. Assuming that your child has no other income, this $600 escapes income tax each year.

On your son's 18th birthday, twelve years after the original investment, you turn over to him the $6,000 of principal plus $7,200 of accumulated tax-free income (plus any interest earned on this amount).

Had you merely registered the securities in your own name

and not as custodian for John, you would have paid a 50% tax on your income, leaving only $3,600 of accumulated income for your son.

There is an added income tax advantage. Even though you, as custodian, accumulate a substantial amount of income for the ultimate benefit of your child, the child remains your dependent for tax purposes.

HOW TO PLAN SALES TO CLOSE RELATIVES

Sales to close relatives are subject to special tax rules which must be carefully reviewed to avoid tax penalties.

If you are planning to sell securities or property to a relative, following all the legal technicalities and setting a fair price for the item may not avoid certain tax restrictions. A rule prevents you from deducting a loss incurred on a sale made to your spouse, children, parents, grandparents, brother, or sister. If you want to claim a loss deduction, you have to sell to someone else.

EXAMPLES—

1. A real estate investor sells a lot to his sister for $2000. It cost him $5000. He may not deduct the $3000 loss even though the sale was made in good faith and the price was fair.

2. A husband and wife each own stock which declined in value. They wanted to realize the losses for tax purposes but were unwilling to sell unless they could keep their position in the stock. The husband bought on the New York Stock Exchange an identical number of shares of the same stock that his wife owned; his wife bought an identical number of shares of the same stock that he owned. The next day each sold the stock originally owned. Their losses were disallowed. The IRS held that the couple had made indirect sales between themselves and the losses were not deductible. Making the sales in the open market was immaterial.

If you want to sell to your sister, you cannot avoid the loss rules by making the sale to your brother-in-law, a nominee of your sister. This sale is deemed to be between you and your sister. However, a bona fide sale to your brother-in-law or any other in-law would qualify for the deduction.

MAKE LOANS TO RELATIVES AND FRIENDS

When you help out a friend or relative, you may be inclined to overlook business formalities. If you are concerned about repayment and the possibility of claiming a bad debt deduction, you must proceed differently.

If you make a personal loan to a relative or friend, you probably will not charge interest and may pass the funds without the signing of a note. And if the friend or relative cannot repay, you may not press for payment. The IRS is aware of these sentiments when a person tries to deduct a bad debt loss for a family loan. It disallows the deduction, claiming the lender intended a gift, not a loan. If you are concerned about repayment of a loan to a friend or relative and the possibility of claiming a bad debt deduction, you should go through the formalities of a business loan by taking a note and setting a time for payment. Finally, if you do not receive payment, make an attempt to collect the amount due you. Failure to try to collect on a family debt may be viewed in court as evidence of a gift, even if you have gone through the formalities of taking a note and charging interest.

There is also a tax risk in not charging interest if the loan is over $10,000 or the relative uses a loan of $10,000 or less to buy or carry investments. In such a case, the loan may be considered a taxable gift and you may be treated as receiving taxable income for imputed interest.

EMPLOY CHILDREN IN A FAMILY BUSINESS

Income may be shifted to children you employ in your business. Their pay is deductible as a business expense as long as it is reasonable and for actual services.

Employing children in a family-run business has two tax advantages. Wages paid to the children will be taxed in their low tax brackets, and you or the family company that is the employer may deduct the children's wages as a business expense. The IRS may be suspicious of deductions claimed for children's wages and may disallow them, claiming that the pay exceeds the value of services rendered. Be prepared to support the deductions with proof that the children actually worked for their pay.

Pay must be reasonable to be deductible. Do not expect the IRS to allow as reasonable the same amount of wages to a ten-year-old as to a teenager. If a child's pay is increased from one year to the next, be prepared to show that he or she did extra work warranting the increase.

For example, Eller paid his three children for doing odd jobs, such as landscaping, cleaning, and making deliveries for his mobile home business. His seven-year-old son was paid almost as much as the two older children, ages 11 and 12. The IRS held that Eller could not deduct anything for the youngest child's services and could only deduct $1,800 of the $12,545 paid to the older children over three years. However, the Tax Court allowed Eller to deduct most of the children's pay; only $2,150 was disallowed. Eller was not allowed to deduct as much for the youngest child as for the older children. Further, he could not deduct a portion of the salary increases over the three-year period because there was no evidence that the children did any extra work warranting the raises.

Warning: In figuring tax savings, do not ignore the cost of payroll tax costs on wages paid to children.

DEDUCT EXPENSES OF A SIDELINE BUSINESS

Hobbies have often turned into profitable businesses. But frequently during the turnaround, losses may be incurred for several years. Planning can help you deduct these losses.

As a practical matter, the question of whether an activity, such as dog breeding or collecting and selling coins and stamps, is a hobby or a sideline business arises when losses are incurred. As long as you show a profit, you may deduct the expenses of the activity. But when expenses exceed income and your return is examined, an agent may allow expenses only up to the amount of your income and disallow the remaining expenses that make up your loss. You should anticipate such a confrontation and prepare your strongest case. You should be able to prove that you operate in a businesslike manner and keep complete and accurate books and records. When necessary, show that you have used the expertise of leaders in the field to give you advice. You should show the amount of time and effort you have spent carrying on the activity and your expectation that your assets used in the activity may appreciate in value and that you will make a profit. Demonstrating a profit in two or more years during a five-year period will help. If you can show this, the law presumes that you are in an activity for profit. Even if you cannot show these profits but you anticipate profits in later years, you have this option: You may elect to delay a determination of the loss deduction issue until the fifth taxable year from the year you first entered the activity. If you then realize at least two profitable years, the presumption of profit will apply to the loss years. You make the election on a special form obtained from the IRS. In making the election, you sign a waiver of the statute of limitations for the taxable years involved. The waiver generally does not apply to unrelated items on your return and allows the IRS to assess deficiencies related to the activity for the open years. In the case of horse racing, breeding, or showing, the presumption based on two profitable years is measured during a seven-year period.

The election may be made within three years of the due date of the return for the year in which you started your activity. If during this period you do not make an election and your return is examined, you may make the election within 60 days from the date you receive a deficiency notice disallowing your loss deduction.

Even if you file the election, the IRS may rebut this presumption. If it does, you must then show facts that support your claim of being engaged in an activity for profit. Similarly, if you do not show two profitable years in the five-year period, you may have to prove your case by showing facts in your favor.

CLAIM HOME OFFICE EXPENSES

Employees have few opportunities to deduct home office expenses unless they have a sideline business or are required by their job to meet clients at home or receive calls from them.

You may have an occupation and also manage rental property or run a sideline business from an office in your home. The home office expenses are deductible if it is the principal place of operating the rental or sideline business. For example, you have a full-time job but also own rental properties which you personally manage. Set up one room of your house to use exclusively as an office to manage the properties. Furnish it with a desk, filing cabinet, and answering service. You may deduct expenses allocable to the home office.

If you cannot set aside a whole room as an office, you may use a partition to separate an office from the rest of the room you use for other purposes, such as a bedroom. The IRS does not require a physical partition but if you do not physically divide the room into business and personal areas, it will be more difficult to prove that part of your home is used exclusively as an office.

In claiming home office expenses of a sideline business, it is also important to be able to prove that you are actually in business. A court has held that activities related to seeking new tenants, supplying furnishings, and cleaning and preparing units for tenants are sufficiently systematic and continuous to put a person in the business of real estate rental. In some cases the rental of even a single piece of real property may be a business. However, investors managing their securities portfolio may find it next to impossible to convince a court that reading financial services and making investment decisions is a business activity.

In another case, an appeals court provides a basis for musicians and others with similar occupational needs for proving that their home may be their principal place of business. According to the court, a concert musician who must practice at home to maintain his skills may deduct the expenses of a practice area in his home. Helpful to the musician's case was the fact that his employer did not provide facilities for practice.

SHOULD YOU SUBLET, ASSIGN, OR SEEK CANCELLATION OF A LEASE?

Tax consequences may influence the way in which you, as tenant, dispose of a lease.

Before deciding whether to sublet, assign, or seek cancellation of a lease, compute whether the rental value of the premises is greater or less than the rent required by your lease.

If you can get more for the premises than you are obligated to pay, try to assign the lease. You might base your price on the present value of the increased rental during the remaining term of the lease. A profit realized on the assignment is generally taxable as capital gain if you held the lease long term and are not in the business of marketing leases. But note: If your lease is a depreciable asset used in your business, your right to capital gain is affected by the disposition of other assets used in your business. If you sublet rather than assign your lease, your profit, as rentals continue to be received over the remaining lease term, is taxable as ordinary income. Therefore an assignment at capital gain rates is preferable to ordinary income realized on subletting. If your landlord is willing to pay you a bonus to cancel your lease, your profit is also taxable at capital gain rates just as if you had sold the lease to a third party.

If the present rental value of business premises is less than your primary rent obligation, try to negotiate a lease cancellation with your landlord in return for your payment of a fixed sum. You can deduct the amount in the year it is paid. If you sublet to a third party at a loss, you have to spread the loss over the term of the sublease as rentals are received. If you assign the lease and pay the assignee an amount to compensate for the assumption of the higher primary rent obligation, your payment is likewise spread over the remaining term of the lease.

The above suggestions generally apply also to the profitable disposition of a lease on a personal apartment or residence. A bonus received on the cancellation or assignment of a personal lease is taxable at capital gain rates if the lease has been held long term. Increased rents received on a sublease are taxable at ordinary income rates. However, losses resulting from the payment of a bonus to landlord in return for the cancellation of a personal lease may not be deducted. Similarly, you may not deduct your payment to an assignee of your lease; nor can you deduct losses on subletting your apartment.

HOW TO PROTECT AN EXEMPTION FOR SUPPORTING A MARRIED CHILD

Plan with your married dependent how to file tax returns for the best family tax break.

Your newly married son or daughter may need your financial help to start a household. You may in fact be providing more than half of the couple's support. If you are, you may be able to claim them as exemptions, but not if they file a joint return. You may not claim an exemption for a dependent who files a joint return with another. For example, you meet all of the tests entitling you to an exemption for your married daughter as your dependent. She files a joint return with her husband. You may not claim her as a dependent on your tax return.

The loss of the exemption may cost you more than the joint return saves the couple. In such a case it may be advisable for them to file separate returns so that you may benefit from the larger tax saving. To convince them, figure the tax savings from your exemption claim and compare it with the tax savings, if any, they get by filing jointly over filing separately.

If the couple has filed a joint return and decides to revoke their election in order to preserve the exemption for you, they must do so before the filing date for the return. Once a joint return is filed, a separate return for the same year may not be filed after the filing deadline has passed.

The IRS allows a limited opportunity for avoiding the rule that no exemption may be claimed for a dependent filing a joint return. If the income of each spouse is under the income limit required for filing a return and the couple files a joint return merely to obtain a refund of withheld taxes, their return is considered a refund claim and a dependency exemption may be claimed.

HOW TO PLAN SUPPORT FOR SEVERAL DEPENDENTS

Do you help support several relatives? You may have to take steps to protect your dependency exemptions.

If you are contributing funds to a household of several persons and the amount you contribute does not exceed 50% of the total support cost of the household, you may be able to claim an exemption for at least one dependent by earmarking your support to his or her use if your contribution will exceed 50% of support costs. You may do this by marking your checks for the benefit of the department, or by preparing a statement of your support arrangement at the time you start your payments. The IRS will generally accept such evidence of your arrangement. If you do not designate the person you are supporting, your contribution is allocated equally among all members of the household.

For example, you live apart from your family without a legal separation and send your wife $2,100 annually to meet household expenses. Your son and daughter live with her. Your wife contributes $4,200 annually from her own funds; her father sends her $900. The total amount to meet household expenses from all sources is $7,200. On a separate return you may not claim any exemptions for the children; your contributions are less than 50% of their total support. Since you have not ear-

	Allocated to:			
Contributed by:	Wife	Son	Daughter	Total
Wife	$1400	$1400	$1400	$4200
You	700	700	700	2100
Wife's Father	300	300	300	900
Total	$2400	$2400	$2400	$7200

marked who is to receive your contributions, your payments are allocated equally among the three members of the household. Each is considered to have received $700 from you, which is less than half of the total support of $2,400 ($7,200 ÷ 3) allocated to each member of the household.

Now, assume you note on your monthly checks of $175 that $105 is for your son and $70 for your daughter. You may claim your son as an exemption on a separate return; you have contributed more than half of his support.

	Allocated to:			
Contributed by:	Wife	Son	Daughter	Total
Wife	$2100	$ 840	$1260	$4200
You		1260	840	2100
Father	300	300	300	900
Total	$2400	$2400	$2400	$7200

If you and others share the support of one person but no one gives more than 50%, the tax law allows you to decide among yourselves who is to claim the exemption. You can claim the exemption if you gave more than 10% of the dependent's support and get multiple support agreements from the others who each gave more than 10% and have decided to let you take the exemption. For example, you and your sister contribute $2,000 each toward the support of your mother. She contributes $1,000 to her own support. Your two brothers contribute $500 each. Thus the total support comes to $6,000. Of this, you and your sister each gave 33% ($2,000/$6,000) for a total of 66%. Each brother gave 8.3% ($500/$6,000), which is less than 10%. You or your sister may claim the exemption. The total of your contributions is more than half of your mother's support. Each of you contributed more than 10%. Between yourselves you must decide who is to claim the exemption. If you claim the exemption, your sister must sign Form 2120, which you attach to your return. If your sister claims the exemption, you sign Form 2120, which is attached to her return. Since neither of your brothers furnished more than 10%, neither can claim the exemption. Consequently they need not sign Form 2120.

16

TAX PLANNING FOR MARITAL BREAKUPS

By taking tax rules into consideration, you, with your professional counselors, can arrange beforehand how the costs of a divorce are to be borne.

Divorces and legal separations involve property settlements, alimony, and support payments. If the parties agree that one spouse (usually the husband) is to pay deductible alimony and the other (usually the wife) is to report the alimony as income, these rules must be met:

1. Payments are in cash.
2. The parties do not live in the same household if they are legally separated under a decree of divorce or separate maintenance.
3. Liability for alimony ends on the death of the payee-spouse.
4. Payments over $10,000 must continue for at least six years unless either spouse dies beforehand or the payee-spouse remarries.

Recapture. If during the six-year period, payments decrease by more than $10,000 from payments in a prior year, the payer must recapture prior alimony deductions and report the amount as income. No recapture applies to any year in which payments terminated because of the death of either spouse or the remarriage of the payee.

EXAMPLE—

Under a decree entered in 1985, Jones pays and deducts alimony payments of $25,000. In 1986, he pays only $12,000. In 1986, $3,000 of the deduction of the prior year is recaptured. Jones' ex-spouse may also claim a $3,000 deduction.

1985 deduction		$25,000
Less:		
Payments in 1986	$12,000	
Plus $10,000	10,000	22,000
Recapture		$ 3,000

The recapture rule does not apply to payments made under an instrument that requires the payment over a period of at least six years of a fixed portion of the income from a business from property or from compensation for employment or self-employment.

Child support. Payments specified as or related to child support are not taxable or deductible as alimony. For example, if the amount to be paid is reduced upon an event related to the child (such as reaching a specific age, leaving school, dying or marrying), the payment is treated as child support to the extent of the reduction. If both alimony and child support are specified, any payment less than the total of the two amounts is first allocated to child support.

Figure the tax cost of each alternative; your lawyer will draft documents supporting your agreement. Understanding and settling the legal and tax consequences of marital disputes can avoid costly personal and tax disputes in the future.

If you are to receive taxed alimony, you may deduct part of your legal fees. Ask your attorney to divide the fees into charges for arranging the separation and divorce and charges for arranging the details of the alimony payments. You may deduct the legal fees allocated to the latter, but you may not deduct the fee attributed to the separation or divorce negotiation. If alimony is not taxed to you, you may not deduct any part of the fee. However, part of a fee allocated to a property settlement may be added to the basis of property obtained in the settlement.

You may not deduct legal fees paid for arranging a divorce or for resisting your spouse's demands for alimony. Furthermore, you may not deduct legal fees incurred in resisting your spouse's claims to income-producing property, the loss of which would affect your earnings. However, you may deduct the part of the legal fee that is identified as being for tax advice.

Property transfers incident to divorce. A marital settlement may involve transfers of property between the spouses. Under pre-1985 law, the transferor could be subject to taxable gain. Under a new law, tax-free exchange rules apply to transfers made after July 18, 1984 between spouses or between former spouses where the transfer is incident to a divorce. For a transfer to a former spouse to be considered "incident to a divorce," it must either occur within one year after the date the marriage ceases or it must be related to the cessation of the marriage, such as where the transfer is authorized by a divorce decree. The tax-free exchange rule does not apply to transfers to a present spouse who is a non-resident alien but it does apply if the transfer is to a former spouse who is a non-resident alien, provided that the "incident to a divorce" time test is met.

Under the new rule, the transfer is treated as a gift so that the basis of the property in the hands of the transferee-spouse is the same as the basis of the property in the hands of the transferor-spouse.

EXAMPLE—

In a property settlement incident to a divorce, a husband plans to transfer to his wife stock worth $20,000 which cost him $5,000. In deciding whether to agree to the transfer, the wife should be aware that her basis for the stock will be $5,000; if she sells the stock, she will have to pay tax on the $15,000 gain. She should consider this tax cost in arriving at the settlement.

TAX BREAKS FOR SINGLE PARENTS

Single parents are entitled to tax breaks to ease the high cost of maintaining a household. Check which tax status will result in the greatest savings.

Single parents can pay less tax by taking advantage of special rates allowed them, depending on their current tax status. When you file your return, select the tax status which gives you the lowest tax. Your status is determined as of the last day of the year. If your spouse died recently, you may still be able to use joint-return rates. If you are a widow or widower and your spouse died in 1982 or 1983, you may figure your 1984 tax using joint-return rates if you meet these four tests: (1) you maintain your home as the main home of your child, adopted child, or stepchild for the entire year, and you furnish over half the cost of maintaining the household; (2) you are entitled to claim the child as a dependent; (3) in the year your spouse died, you could have filed a joint return under the rules above; (4) you did not remarry before January 1, 1985.

If you cannot meet these rules, you still might pay less tax by qualifying as head of household if you meet these five tests: (1) you are not married at the end of the year; (2) you maintain a household for the entire year for your child or a dependent relative; (3) the household must be your home and the main residence of a dependent relative for the whole tax year if you claim head of household rates in 1984. For 1985, the residence period is reduced to more than half of the year. (A dependent parent need not live in your home); you pay more than one-half the cost of the household you maintain; (5) you are a U.S. citizen or resident alien during the entire tax year.

Make sure you can prove that your dependent unmarried child lives with you in your principal residence for the entire year. You must also pay more than one-half the cost of the household you maintain. The costs of maintaining a household include: property taxes, mortgage interest, rent, utility charges, upkeep and repairs, domestic help, property insurance, and food eaten in the household. You do not consider the rental value of the lodgings provided the dependent, as in the case of figuring support for a dependency exemption. Also not included in the cost of maintaining a household are: clothing, education costs, medical expenses, vacation costs, life insurance premiums, transportation costs, and the value of your work around the house.

A divorced or separated couple who share the support of a dependent child may decide who is to claim the exemption. Starting in 1985, the custodial parent has first claim to the exemption but may waive it by signing a declaration. The waiver does not affect the custodial parent's right to claim head of household status, the earned-income credit, or the child-care credit. The noncustodial parent must attach the waiver declaration to his or her return to claim the exemption. Each parent may treat the children as dependents for purposes of deducting the children's medical costs.

TAX BENEFITS OF WINNING SCHOLARSHIPS

Scholarships may be the only way families can afford to send their children to college and other higher studies. Tax benefits increase the value of qualified scholarships.

Your children should be encouraged to apply for scholarships and other educational grants. Scholarship aid to your children will help pay the current high costs of education, and at the same time, the scholarship aid given them does not prevent you from claiming them as dependents if you provide the balance of their support. Scholarship aid is not counted as support contribution. For example, your son receives scholarship aid amounting to $3,500 a year, and you give him spending money of $1,000. You can claim him as a dependent even though in fact you did not provide over 50% of his support. The law allows you to ignore the scholarship, provided your child is a full-time student for at least five calendar months during the year. If your child attends an accredited nursing school, the value of food and lodging may also be ignored.

Also, your child may not be taxed on scholarship aid if he or she is a degree candidate. The following amounts paid under a grant are tax free: tuition, matriculation fees, room, board, laundry and other services, and family allowances.

Payments in a work-study program are tax free if the college requires all its students to take part. Payments for services not required by the program are taxable.

A child is not taxed on allowances specifically designated for expenses incident to the grant, such as costs of travel (including meals and lodging while traveling and family travel allowance), research, clerical help, and equipment. You are taxable to the extent the allowance is not spent for these purposes.

If the primary purpose of teaching or research is to further the child's own training and education, payment for such services is tax free if the services are required of all degree candidates.

If the child is not working for a degree, a scholarship or fellowship grant is tax free up to $300 a month for each month during the year in which he or she receives payments under the grant. The child may claim the $300-a-month exclusion for only 36 months during your lifetime. The months do not have to be consecutive. A grant does not qualify for this tax-free exclusion if it represents payment for services or for research or studies primarily for the grantor's benefit.

TAX SAVINGS IN HOME OWNERSHIP

Deductions for property taxes and mortgage interest often make home ownership a better economic choice than renting.

The tax laws favor home ownership. The direct tax benefits provided homeowners are deductions allowed for real estate taxes and interest on your mortgage. The following example will illustrate how tax savings reduce the cost of home ownership: Assume you have the option of renting an apartment for $1,000 monthly or buying a house. If you buy the house, your annual costs will be $9,000 in interest, $2,400 in taxes, and nondeductible charges of $600. Assume further that your other itemized deductions exceed your zero bracket amount; the net cost of house ownership will be:

If your bracket is	Net annual cost of home ownership is
25%	$9150
33%	$8238
38%	$7668
42%	$7212
45%	$6870
50%	$6300

Assuming comparative rental charges of $12,000 a year and no unusual costs involving unexpected home repairs, the above figures show that home ownership is by far the better financial deal.

The tax benefits of home ownership are not limited to single-family homes; you may deduct your taxes and interest on a condominium or cooperative apartment.

There is also another advantage to home ownership. If your property increases in value, you can sell and defer tax on your profit by buying another residence. If you are 55 or over, you can take advantage of a one-time election to avoid tax on up to $125,000 of your profit.

USE TAX CREDITS TO DEFRAY COSTS OF HOME ENERGY IMPROVEMENTS

Save on your home heating costs by using tax credits to defray costs of certain home improvements.

The costs of heating and cooling your home, while not escalating as rapidly as in the past decade, will continue to increase. Cost effectiveness dictates insulating and making other energy-saving improvements to your home. To save on out-of-pocket expenses, you may reduce your tax bill by as much as 40% of the cost of solar-energy devices or 15% of insulation and other improvements. In addition, most states offer tax incentives, whether as deductions, credits, or property tax exemptions, to stimulate energy-saving improvements.

The federal tax law has two distinct credits: a credit for energy-conservation expenditures, such as insulation, and a credit for renewable-energy-source expenditures, such as solar-energy conductors. The credits are figured separately.

A 15% credit on expenditures up to $2,000 (for a maximum credit of $30) may be claimed for an original installment of insulation and other energy-conserving components with a useful life of at least three years. The credit applies to your payments for: (1) insulation for ceilings, walls, floors, roofs, and water heaters; (2) furnace replacement burner, designed to reduce the amount of fuel consumed as a result of increased combustion efficiency (the burner must replace an existing burner; it does not qualify if it is acquired as a component of, or for use in, a new furnace or boiler); (3) a device for modifying flue openings in heating systems which increase efficiency; (4) an electrical or mechanical furnace-ignition system which replaces a gas pilot light; (5) storm or thermal windows or doors for the exterior of a dwelling; (6) automatic energy-saving setback thermostats; (7) caulking and weather-stripping of an exterior door or window; and (8) a meter which displays the cost of energy usage.

Home improvements not qualifying for the credit are: carpeting, drapes, and wood paneling; exterior siding (such as aluminum siding); heat pumps; wood- or heat-fueled residential equipment (which includes fireplaces and woodburning stoves); fluorescent replacement lighting systems; replacement boilers and furnaces; air conditioners, heat reclaimers; power factor improvers; attic or whole house fans; films or coatings applied to surface of windows or doors; greenhouses; expenditures for a swimming pool used as an energy storage medium; and hydrogen-fueled residential equipment.

A credit of 40% of expenditures up to $10,000 (for a maximum credit of $4,000) may be claimed for solar, wind, or geothermal devices, or devices from other renewable-energy sources which provide hot water or electricity for use in the home or for heating or cooling the home. You must be the original user of the unit, and the unit must be reasonably expected to last for at least five years.

Both active and passive systems qualify for the renewable-energy-source credit. An active solar-energy system is based on the use of mechanically forced energy transfer, such as the use of fans or pumps to circulate solar-generated energy; a passive solar-energy system is based on the use of conductive, convective, or radiant energy transfer. A passive solar energy system must contain all of the following: (1) a solar collection area; (2) an absorber; (3) a storage mass; (4) a heat distribution method; and (5) a heat regulation device. Materials and components of a solar-energy system that have a significant structural function or are structural components of a residence do not qualify as solar-energy property. An exception is made for solar roof panels which qualify for the credit.

The special energy credits apply only to improvements made before the end of 1985.

KEEP ACCOUNTS OF IMPROVEMENTS TO YOUR RESIDENCE

You may lose tax benefits if you do not keep records of your home costs and improvements.

The time span of home ownership may cover decades, and unless you keep records you may be unable to report adequately the sale of the house. By failing to keep track of home improvements you may overstate the amount of your gain.

Your records should include the purchase price of your house plus fees paid for title insurance, recording fees, transfer taxes, and legal fees. Also, bills or other records detailing capital improvements made to the house for additional rooms, equipment, landscaping, and similar capital items. The basis of your old house is the total cost shown by these records. If you deducted a casualty loss for damage to your house, the basis of the house should be reduced by the amount deducted. If you claimed an energy credit, you do not increase the basis by the amount of the credit.

When you sell the house, make sure you have: (1) the sales contract showing the sales price of the house; (2) a statement showing settlement costs at the closing and allocating taxes and fire insurance; (3) the bill and record of payment of legal fees; (4) record of payment of broker's fees, if any; (5) a closing statement from the bank holding the mortgage on your old house showing final interest charges up to the date of transfer of title and prepayment penalties, if any; (6) if you incurred fix-up costs, records of when the work was done and when payment was made; and (7) a record of payments for advertising the sale of the house, if any.

You reduce the selling price of the house by payments for broker's commissions, legal fees, and advertising expenses. Paying off the principal balance of the mortgage to the bank does not enter into the tax computation. If you buy a new house, you should have your contract showing the cost of the new house plus any additional improvements and the closing statement showing title insurance fees, adjustment of taxes, mortgage fees, and recording fees.

The cost basis of your new house includes the purchase price (even though all or part is covered by a mortgage), attorney's fees, mortgage fees, title insurance fees, and recording fees, less the gain not taxed on the sale of your old home.

If you purchased your house after selling a house on which you deferred tax, you should also keep a record of the costs of the prior house and the tax return on which you elected to defer tax. The basis of the current house must reflect the basis of the prior house.

MAKE THE MOST OF THE $125,000 RESIDENCE EXCLUSION

You have a once-in-a-lifetime opportunity to avoid tax on the profitable sale of your house. It may not be advisable to claim it on your first sale.

If you are age 55 or over and considering a sale of your principal residence, the tax law allows you to make a once-in-a-lifetime election to avoid tax on up to $125,000 of profit. But you might not want to elect the exclusion in certain situations. Perhaps you expect to sell your principal residence at a gain which is substantially less than $125,000, and you plan to re-invest all of the net proceeds from the sale in a new home or condominium. It is preferable to defer tax under the regular tax law rules rather than electing to exclude gain under the $125,000 exclusion. For example, if you realize gain of $40,000 on the sale of your residence and make an election to exclude it from income, you have used up your once-in-a-lifetime election; a later home sale will not be entitled to the unused portion of the $125,000 exclusion. But if you buy a new home within two years before or after the sale of your old house or condominium at a cost which is at least equal to the adjusted sales price of the old home, you have deferred tax on the entire gain from the sale of your old home and need not make an election to avoid tax under the $125,000 exclusion. Later, you may be ready to sell the new house without a further home purchase and the election to exclude gain may then be made.

If your gain exceeds $125,000, you might be able to combine the exclusion with tax deferral. You may consider electing the exclusion to shelter your gain up to $125,000 and buy a new residence to defer all or part of the remaining gain, depending on the amount of the investment in the new home. You can defer all of the remaining gain by making an investment at least equal to the adjusted sales price of the old house (sales price less selling expenses and fix-up costs), less the $125,000 tax-free gain. For example, say you are over age 55 and sell your home realizing $200,000 gain. You may use the one-time exclusion to avoid tax on $125,000 of your profit. If within two years you buy another home that costs at least $75,000 (the difference between your gain and the $125,000 exclusion), you avoid tax on the sale. If you buy a second home for less than $75,000, you are taxed on the difference between the price of the new home and your gain on the sale of your old home, less the $125,000 exclusion. However, you are taxed only to the extent of the remaining gain.

Married couples should be particularly aware of the tax rules applying to the exclusion. Only one lifetime election is allowed to a married couple; each spouse does not have a separate election.

If you are single and have not made an election but are considering a sale of your home in contemplation of marriage, you may have to sell the house before marrying if your intended spouse has already made the election. Marital status is determined at the time of sale. Take this example: John sold his home at a profit in August 1984 and elected on his 1984 return to avoid tax. Grace, his intended wife, has not yet sold her home on which she anticipates substantial profit. They plan to marry in 1985. If she sells the home before the wedding, she has the right to claim the exclusion for herself since she is not yet John's wife. However, if sale of the house is deferred and the marriage takes place first, the 1984 election by John would prevent an exclusion for Grace. Once married, her right to claim the election on the sale of her home is forfeited by John's prior election, although his sale took place before their marriage. Under these circumstances, it would clearly be good tax sense for Grace's house sale to be completed before the marriage takes place.

TAKE A PURCHASE-MONEY MORTGAGE TO CLOSE A SALE OF YOUR HOME

If a potential buyer of your house cannot obtain adequate mortgage financing from a bank, you may be able to close the sale by taking a purchase-money mortgage.

During the current period of high interest rates, many persons interested in buying homes have been unable to get adequate mortgage financing. To prevent deals from falling through, some sellers have been willing to finance the sale by allowing the buyer to pay in installments. This is called a purchase-money mortgage. The buyer signs installment notes for the outstanding purchase price. The purchase is secured by the house and the seller can foreclose if installment payments are not made.

For tax purposes, when you take back a purchase-money mortgage, you have made an installment sale. Part of each payment made by the buyer is reported as taxable gain. To determine the amount of each payment taxable as income, you apply the gross profit ratio to each payment actually received. The gross profit ratio is figured by dividing the taxable gain by the total contract price. If you have made a $60,000 gain on a home sold for $100,000, you have a profit ratio of 60%, and 60% of each payment you receive over the years from the buyer is taxable and reported as gain.

Interest. The tax law requires a minimum amount of interest to be charged on a deferred payment sale.

If the amount borrowed from the seller is $2 million or less on a sale from January 1 through June 30, 1985, interest of at least 9% compounded semiannually must be charged. Otherwise, interest at a rate of 10% compounded semiannually is imputed. If the seller-financed amount exceeds $2 million, a larger "blended" rate is imputed.

On the sale of a principal residence for $250,000 or less after June 30, 1985, at least 9% simple interest must be charged. Otherwise, the IRS imputes interest at 10% compounded semiannually. If the sale price is over $250,000, interest is imputed under original issue discount rules. To the extent the price exceeds $250,000, you must charge at least 110% of a federal rate (short-term, mid-term, or long-term, depending on the length of the contract), compounded semiannually. If you charge less, the imputed interest rate is 120% of the applicable federal rate, compounded semiannually. The rate for sales after June 30, 1985 was not available when this book was published.

Later, you may be interested in selling or giving away the installment note. If you exchange or sell the note at other than face value, gain or loss results to the extent of the difference between the basis of the note and the amount realized. Gain or loss is long term if the original sale was entitled to long-term capital gain treatment.

What if the buyer defaults and you repossess the house? Gain on the repossession is the excess of:

1. Payments received on the original sales contract prior to and on the repossession, over
2. The amount of taxable gain previously reported prior to the repossession.

Gain computed under these two steps may not be fully taxable. Taxable gain is limited to the amount of original profit less gain on the sale already reported as income for periods prior to the repossession and less your repossession costs.

If your original sale was not taxed because you deferred gain by reinvesting in another house or you avoided gain under the once-in-a-lifetime exclusion, you do not have to report gain under these rules if you resell the property within one year of repossession. The resale is treated as part of the transaction comprising the original sale.

24

HOW TO DEDUCT A LOSS ON THE SALE OF YOUR HOUSE

The tax law does not allow you to deduct a loss on the sale of a personal residence. If you are facing a substantial loss on the sale of your home, consider renting it instead of selling now.

Renting a home may be considered a changeover to profit-making purposes. If you later sell at a loss, the loss is deductible. However, be aware that merely putting the house up for rent or renting for several months may not be recognized as a conversion to rental property. Nonetheless, one court approved a loss deduction for a house rented on a 90-day lease with an option to buy. The court set down two tests for determining a rental conversion: (1) the rental returned a profit; and (2) the lease kept the owner from reoccupying the house during the lease period. Under this approach, you have a conversion if you have a lease that gives possession of the house to the tenant during the lease period, and the rent returns you a profit after deducting taxes, interest, insurance, repairs, depreciation, and other expenses.

There is also this advantage in renting the house: the delay in selling it may allow you to realize income and perhaps sell at a better price if the market for your house improves.

You may deduct a loss if you rented part of your house and occupied part of it for personal purposes. A loss on a sale is allowable on the rented portion. A loss deduction is also allowed if you acquired the house as an investment with the intention of selling it at a profit even though you occupied it incidentally as a residence prior to sale.

You may deduct a loss on the sale of a house which was received as an inheritance or gift if you personally did not use it and you offered it for sale or rental immediately or within a few weeks after acquisition. If you inherit a residence in which you do not intend to live, it may be advisable to put it up for rent or sale, not for sale alone. If you merely try to sell, and you finally do so at a loss, you are limited to a capital loss. If you first try to rent but cannot, you will probably have an ordinary loss when you finally sell.

HOW TO DEDUCT LOAN FEES

Whether a loan fee is deductible as interest or must be amortized over the life of the loan depends on how you structure the initial transfer of funds.

To secure financing for a realty purchase, the bank or other lender may charge you a loan fee. To get the immediate deduction, you should first obtain the full amount of the loan and then pay the fee to the lender. The deduction is allowed even if the prepayment of interest is an integral part of the loan agreement and the lender would not have made the loan without the fee. However, if the lender gives you only the net proceeds of the loan, no immediate deduction is allowed. You must amortize the fee over the life of the loan.

In one case a borrower claimed that the two methods of structuring a loan have the same economic result. Therefore he should be able to deduct a loan fee even though the bank withheld the fee from proceeds of the loan.

A court agreed that there was no economic difference between the two transactions. Even so, the rule is well settled that no immediate deduction is allowed when the borrower does not receive full principal and does not actually pay the fee to the bank.

USE BORROWED FUNDS TO PAY INTEREST

Do you owe interest on an outstanding debt? To get an interest deduction you must actually pay the interest. You cannot get the deduction by having the creditor add the interest to the debt. If you do not have funds to pay the interest, you may borrow to pay it.

It is advisable to borrow the funds from a different creditor. The IRS objects to a deduction if a debtor borrows from the same creditor to make interest payments on an earlier loan. Its reasoning: When a second loan from the same creditor is used to pay the interest on an earlier loan, no interest has been paid. The second loan is merely a device for getting an interest expense deduction without actually making payments.

Courts tend to side with the IRS. However, the Tax Court has allowed deductions for interest paid with funds borrowed from the same creditor when: (1) there were reasons for the second loan other than to repay interest on the first loan; (2) the borrower could have made the interest payments with other funds; and (3) the proceeds of the second loan actually commingled with the borrower's other funds and were subject to his unrestricted control. However, be aware that this favorable approach may not be followed by other courts. This was the experience of a real estate developer. Each quarter he would send the bank a check for interest due on an earlier loan used to purchase property and the bank would reimburse him for his payment with its own check. The developer claimed that the additional loans gave him financial flexibility; he had ample assets to cover the interest charges, but he did not want to use these funds for interest payments. The developer deducted the interest payments, which the IRS disallowed. A federal district court allowed the deduction. An appeals court reversed. The developer merely promised payment of the interest in the future, plus additional interest. This method of deferring interest payments may make business sense, but it does not support an interest deduction. To get the deduction, funds should be borrowed from another lender.

HOW TO FIGURE THE COST OF LEGAL FEES BEFORE YOU SUE

Legal costs for a difficult and protracted case may be substantial. In figuring whether to sue, you should not only consider the chances of recovery but also whether you can deduct legal costs. If you can, the cost of litigation may be materially reduced.

A legal expense is generally deductible if the dispute or issue arose in the course of your business or employment or involves income-producing property. Legal expenses for personal matters are generally not deductible. Determining the line between business and personal matters has led to some legal hair-splitting. For example, the cost of contesting suspension of a driver's license for drunken driving is not deductible, despite a business need for the license; the IRS and the courts have held that a suspension arose out of a personal, rather than a business-related, activity.

A deduction may also be disallowed if the dispute involves title to property. Further, the deductibility of a legal expense may depend on whether the damages received are taxable or not. For example, payments for physical injuries, whether compensatory or punitive, resulting from an automobile accident are tax free. Therefore, an attorney's fees to secure the award are nondeductible. However, if payment is also received for lost wages which would be taxable, the portion of attorney's fees allocable to the taxable payments is deductible.

Matrimonial actions. Legal expenses incurred in marital actions are generally not deductible. However, if a spouse retains an attorney to secure taxable alimony, a portion of that spouse's legal fees allocable to the taxable alimony award is deductible. However, the spouse who is obligated to pay the alimony may not deduct his payment of his former spouse's legal fees allocated to the taxable payments.

Libel suits. According to the IRS, if the libel action is for damage to business reputation, legal expenses are deductible as business expenses. Compensatory damages received in settlement of a libel suit for injury to personal reputation are tax free. Thus legal expenses allocable to the amount received as compensatory damages are not deductible. However, punitive damages for injury to personal reputation are taxable income; legal costs allocable to punitive damages are deductible.

Will contests and wrongful death actions. In general, legal costs of a will contest are not deductible because an inheritance is not taxable. Similarly, legal fees incurred to collect a wrongful death award, which is tax-free income, are not deductible. For example, an heir who was left out of his grandmother's estate sued to recover his inheritance. In a settlement, he received his share of his grandmother's property, plus income earned on that property. The allocable portion of legal fees attributed to the income, which was taxable, was deductible; the balance of the fee was not deductible.

Title issues or disputes. Legal costs related to the acquisition of property or to the determination of title to property, whether or not such property is business or personal, are nondeductible capital expenditures. They are added to the basis of the property. For example, legal fees in litigation fixing the value of shares of dissident shareholders were not deductible because they were related to the purchase of the stock and were part of the cost of acquisition.

Legal fees incurred to quiet title to stock are also nondeductible.

Where a dispute over property does not involve title, such as in a recovery of income-producing securities loaned as collateral, the Tax Court holds that legal fees are deductible.

Legal fees for tax advice, tax return preparation, and tax disputes. You may deduct legal fees charged for preparing your tax return or refund claim, or for representing you in a trial, examination, or hearing involving any tax. Legal fees incurred in defending against a tax imposed by a foreign country are also deductible. However, legal fees incurred in reducing an assessment on real property to pay for local benefits are not deductible; the fees are capital expenses which are added to basis.

Not all of an attorney's fee for estate tax planning services is deductible. Estate tax planning usually involves tax and nontax matters. To the extent that the services do not cover tax advice or income-producing property, the fee is not deductible. A bill allocating a fee between deductible and nondeductible services may help support a deduction claimed for the deductible portion of the fee. Take this case: Estate planning for a doctor involved the drawing of wills, trusts, property transfers, and gift tax returns. The doctor deducted the lawyer's entire fee of $2,000. The IRS disallowed the deduction because the fee was not allocated between tax and nontax matters. The Tax Court viewed the IRS's position as a concession that fees are deductible to the extent allocable to tax advice in estate planning. All the doctor failed to do was to show how much of the fee was for tax advice which the majority of the Tax Court calculated for him. It figured from the evidence that 20% of the attorney's time was spent on tax matters and so allowed a deduction of 20% of the bill.

Make sure that your bills for legal services show the different aspects of the attorney's work. Your lawyer should bill you separately or itemize fees for services connected with deductible items (collection of taxable alimony or separate maintenance payments, preparation of tax returns, tax audits, and tax litigation) and nondeductible capital items (expenses incurred in purchase of property or dispute over title).

For cases begun after February 28, 1983, if you prevail against the IRS in a federal court, including Tax Court and the Claims Court, you may recover attorneys' fees and related costs. You must prove that the government's action was unreasonable. You may recover expenses up to $25,000.

28

EARMARK CARE AND OTHER EXPENSES FOR THE MEDICAL DEDUCTION

There are certain expenses all or part of which may qualify as medical expenses. You have to clearly allocate the medical nature of the expense to get the deduction.

Not all care costs of ill or disabled dependents qualify as medical expenses. However, those that do must be carefully pinpointed by you if they are to be deducted. Here are the problem areas:

Convalescent home costs. A payment for meals and lodging to a nursing home is a deductible medical expense if the patient is confined for medical treatment. Helpful in establishing the full deductibility of payments to these institutions are facts such as: The patient entered the institution on the direction or suggestion of a doctor. Attendance or treatment at the institution had a direct therapeutic effect on the condition suffered by the patient. Attendance at the institution was for a specific ailment rather than for a "general" health condition. That the patient suffers from an ailment is not sufficient proof that he is in the home for treatment.

If you cannot prove that the patient entered the home for medical care (which would permit a deduction for meals and lodging in addition to medical costs), you may nevertheless deduct that part of the cost covering actual medical and nursing care. Have the home separate the various elements of the charges.

Nurses' wages. The costs of a nurse attending an ill person are deductible. Costs include any Social Security (FICA) tax paid by you. That the nurse is not registered or licensed will not bar the deduction, provided the services are performed for the medical aid or treatment of the patient. When you use a nonprofessionally trained person, such as practical nurse, be prepared to show that the nurse performed medical services. If the nurse also performs domestic services, deduct only the pay attributed to medical aid to the patient.

Schooling costs for problem children. You may deduct as medical expenses the costs of sending a mentally or physically handicapped person to a special school or institution to overcome or alleviate his or her handicap. But if you send a problem child to a private school, you can deduct only the fees specifically related to psychological aid given to the child. In such a case it is important for the school to break down the fee, clearly earmarking the costs covering medical care or treatment.

Home equipment for medical care. A disease or ailment may require the construction of special equipment or facilities in a home. You may deduct the full cost of equipment installed for a medical reason if it does not increase the value of your property, for example, the cost of a detachable window air conditioner. If equipment increases the value of your property, you may take a medical deduction to the extent that the cost of the equipment exceeds the increase in the value of the property. To support the deduction, have evidence of the effect of the improvement on your house. If it is a major improvement, it may be advisable to obtain the services of an experienced appraiser.

MEDICAL PLANS FOR FAMILY CORPORATIONS

A simple medical reimbursement plan can allow your company to pay for medical expenses for you and your family.

Medical expenses are not deductible on your return unless they exceed 5% of your adjusted gross income. If you have substantial gross income, you will probably not incur enough medical expenses to exceed this 5% floor. If you are in your own business, you can have your corporation reimburse your medical expenses. The corporation may deduct the payment and you are not taxed on the payments. The company may reimburse you for specific medical expenses which you incurred for yourself, your spouse, or any of your dependents. Or it may pay the expenses directly.

The company may also make tax-free payments for the permanent loss or loss of use of part of the body or for permanent disfigurement of you, your spouse, or a dependent. The payments are based on the kind of injury and have no relation to the length of time you are out of work. These payments are not for medical expenses and are tax free.

Your company plan must be in writing and if it is self-insured must not discriminate in favor of certain highly compensated individuals and stockholders. If reimbursement is provided by an unrelated insurance company, the plan may discriminate in favor of highly compensated executives and stockholders.

If you operate an S corporation, you may be unable to take advantage of a medical plan as an employee-stockholder. For S elections made after September 28, 1982, owners of more than 2% of the stock will realize taxable income for receiving fringe benefit coverage in accident and health plans. However, this tax rule does not apply until 1988 to shareholders of an S corporation existing as of September 28, 1982, provided the corporation does not have passive investment income of more than 20% of gross receipts or does not have a change of majority stockholders after 1982.

TAKE A POSITION THAT HAS FRINGE BENEFITS

High taxes reduce the amount of your take-home pay. A company that offers you tax-free fringe benefits may be offering a better pay package than one that pays you more salary but provides fewer fringe benefits.

Fringe benefits provided by employers increase after-tax income because they are either tax exempt or subject to special tax treatment.

A company qualified pension or profit-sharing plan offers these benefits: (1) you do not realize current income on your employer's contributions to the plan on your behalf; (2) funds contributed by both your employer and you compound tax free within the plan; (3) if you receive a lump sum, tax on employer contributions may be reduced by a special ten-year averaging rule; (4) if you receive a lump-sum distribution in company securities, unrealized appreciation on those securities is not taxed until you sell the stock.

Group insurance plans may furnish not only life insurance protection but accident and health benefits as well. Premium costs paid by your employer are tax free to you unless you have nonforfeitable rights to permanent life insurance, or in the case of group term life insurance, your coverage exceeds $50,000 or the plan is considered discriminatory. Even if your coverage exceeds $50,000, the tax incurred on your employer's premium payment is generally less than the amount you would pay privately for similar insurance.

If you want more insurance than is provided by a group plan, your company may be able to help you obtain additional protection through a split-dollar insurance plan. Under this type of plan your employer purchases permanent life insurance on your life and pays the annual premium to the extent of the yearly increases in the cash surrender value of the policy; you pay only the balance of the premium. At your death your employer is entitled to part of the proceeds equal to the cash surrender value or any lesser amount equaling the total premiums paid.

You have the right to name a beneficiary to receive the remaining proceeds which, under most policies, are substantial compared with the employer's share. You report annually as taxable income an amount equal to the one-year term cost of the declining life insurance protection to which you are entitled less any portion of the premium provided by you.

Companies may provide incentive stock options which are not taxed when granted or exercised. The option spread is taxable as capital gain when the stock is sold.

Starting in 1985, tax law also provides for these four classes of tax-free fringe benefits: (1) services which are provided by the employer to the public which are also offered to employees at no additional cost. These include airline tickets, hotel rooms, and telephone service. Benefits provided by another company under a reciprocal arrangement, such as for standby tickets on another airline, also qualify; (2) employee discounts on goods, such as retail merchandise sold by the employer in the course of business. The exclusion is limited to the seller's gross profit percentage. Also qualifying are discounts on services provided by the employer, with the maximum exclusion limited to 20% of the selling price charged customers. (3) Working condition fringes such as a company car are tax free to the extent that the employee could claim a business expense deduction for the property had he paid for it. (4) So-called "de minimis" fringes which are so small that it would be administratively impractical to tax them.

The exclusions under (1) and (2) are available to officers, owners and other highly compensated employees only if the plan does not discriminate on their behalf.

Tuition reductions for employees (and retired employees) of educational institutions and their families for education below the graduate level are tax free for education furnished after June 30, 1985.

The value of free or low-cost housing provided by universities to faculty members is not specifically provided tax free treatment, but the IRS is barred for two years (through 1985) from writing regulations that would tax the benefits.

DEDUCT COSTS OF JOB HUNTING

You can look for a new job and deduct the costs of your efforts.

You may deduct the expenses of looking for a new job in the same line of work, whether or not a new job is found. Keep a record of your expenses. If you are unemployed when seeking a job, make sure you can show there is no lack of continuity between the past job and the current job search. Deduct the cost of printing resumes and mailing them to prospective employers.

If you travel to find a new job in the same line of work, you may deduct travel expenses, including living costs. If during the trip you also engage in personal activities, you may deduct the transportation expenses if the trip was primarily related to your job search. The primary purpose of your trip is determined by comparing time spent on personal activity to time spent looking for a job. If the transportation expenses to and from your destination are not deductible under this test, you may still deduct expenses allocated to seeking the new job.

If your employer pays an employment agency fee, you may disregard the payment for tax purposes. However, if you pay the fee and after a certain period of employment are reimbursed by your employer, you must report the reimbursement as taxable income. This additional income may be offset by deducting the fee as an itemized deduction.

A company interested in your services may invite you to a job interview and agree to pay all of the expenses of your trip even if you are not hired. The company payment is tax free to the extent that it does not exceed your actual expenses. In addition, the payment is not subject to withholding.

Expenses of seeking a job for the first time are not deductible, even if a job is found.

IMPROVE YOUR JOB SKILLS WITH A TAX WRITE-OFF

Job advancement may depend on further training. The high cost of courses not paid for by your employer can be underwritten by taking courses that qualify for tax deductions.

Courses qualifying for tax deductions may range from refresher courses to advanced academic courses. They may be correspondence school or vocational courses, and even private tutoring.

To qualify for the deduction you must be prepared to show: (1) you are employed or self-employed; (2) you currently meet the minimum requirements of your job, business, or profession; and (3) the course maintains or improves job skills, or you are required by your employer or by law to take the course to keep your present salary or position.

The fact that individuals in positions like yours usually take certain education courses indicates that the courses are taken to maintain and improve job skills. If your employer requires you to obtain further education to retain your present job or rate of pay, you may also deduct the cost of the courses. Your employer's requirement must be for a bona fide business reason, not merely to benefit you. Only the minimum education necessary for the retention of your job or rate of pay is considered by the IRS as meeting your employer's requirement. You must show that any education beyond your employer's minimum requirements is to maintain or improve your job skills.

If your courses qualify, you may deduct (1) the cost of the courses, including tuition, textbooks, fees for equipment and other aids required by the courses; (2) local transportation costs as explained below; (3) travel to and from a school away from home; and (4) living expenses (food and lodging) while at a school away from home. The IRS will not disallow travel expenses to attend a school away from home or in a foreign country merely because you could have taken the course in a local school.

On days you work and attend courses which qualify for an education expense deduction, if your place of employment and school are located within the same general area, you may deduct the cost of travel between your office and school. If you stop at home on your way to school, you may deduct the cost of travel from your home to the school to the extent it does not exceed the cost you would have incurred by going directly from work to school. If your school is located beyond the general area of your principal place of business, you may deduct your round-trip transportation expenses. The cost of traveling between your home and school on a nonworking day is not deductible.

33

DEDUCT COSTS OF TEACHER'S EDUCATIONAL TRAVEL

Travel expenses directly related to teaching are deductible. The educational purpose of the trip and its relation to your position must be carefully documented to support the deduction.

In planning sabbatical or holiday travel, it is advisable to obtain school approval of your travel plans or of the educational objective of your trip. Furthermore, you must actually make the trip an educational venture. Do not rely solely on school approval.

One California couple received school approval for a trip to Hawaii, but by restricting their travel to tourist spots they lost the deduction for the costs of their trip. They enrolled in a graduate course called "World Travel and Academic Enrichment" which required them to develop a proposal for professional objectives for planned travel and to keep a diary for classroom application. As part of the course they and their children spent a Christmas holiday in Hawaii and kept a log of the trip. The IRS, with court approval, disallowed the deduction for travel expenses. It held that their travel was indistinguishable from any other tourist trip. While the trip was approved by their school district and acceptable for professional-growth credits, they failed to show how it had improved their teaching skills. They were, however, allowed to deduct the cost of film, books, records, and other souvenirs which were materials used in their classroom for teaching.

Another teacher failed to qualify for the deduction although her school superintendent certified that she completed the program for which she was granted leave and traveled for the improvement of her teaching skills. She did not show that her trip resulted in a specific improvement of her teaching skills. Following the trip, she merely introduced into her classes dolls, games, and pictures from the trip.

On the other hand an elementary school teacher was allowed to deduct the costs of a European trip. Facts supporting her deduction: Her school board approved the trip as an alternative to taking courses; she turned in a trip report to the school board; she visited museums, which the court held was helpful in teaching art to her pupils.

In another case a high school principal in charge of racial relations in his school and community was allowed to deduct the cost of travel to 44 countries during an approved sabbatical. What the principal learned from the sabbatical was translated into innovative classroom techniques and was shared with other educators and students during seminars following his trip.

Finally, a college professor of physical education was allowed to deduct the cost of a 2½ week visit to the Middle East and Europe. He convinced a court that he spent most of his time studying the history of physical education and athletics in the countries where they originated. He visited museums and libraries and the knowledge he acquired was incorporated in his lectures to students.

34

FIGURE THE BEST WAY TO DEDUCT BUSINESS AUTO COSTS

For the greatest write-off of business use of your car, do not claim the IRS mileage allowance unless your car is exceptionally economical to run or you do a lot of business driving.

If you use your car for business, you have a choice. You may deduct your actual operating costs (plus depreciation) or a flat IRS allowance based on the miles of business travel. You may deduct 20½¢ a mile for the first 15,000 business miles, and 11¢ a mile for mileage over 15,000, plus parking fees and tolls.

Should you claim the IRS allowance? That depends on whether you claim ACRS deductions and the amount of your outlays. You may not claim the mileage allowance if you claim ACRS.

Depending on your business mileage, deductions for ACRS recovery, gasoline, and insurance may exceed the IRS mileage allowance even without accounting for maintenance expenses. The following chart assumes a car used 100% for business with a basis (after the investment credit adjustment) of $8,000, 20 miles per gallon, an average cost of $1.20 per gallon of fuel, and insurance costs of $500.

Business miles	IRS allowance	Actual costs and depreciation
5,000	$1025	$2800
10,000	$2050	$3100
15,000	$3075	$3400
20,000	$3625	$3700
25,000	$4175	$4000

The above comparison does not consider the first-year expensing election. You may elect to deduct up to $4,000 of the cost of a business car instead of recovering that cost through depreciation. If you make the election to expense or claim ACRS, you may not claim the IRS allowance for as long as you own the car.

For autos placed in service after June 18, 1984, new tax rules apply to a 50% business use test, recapture, and annual depreciation ceilings.

More than 50% business use test. If you are an employee, to claim ACRS, first-year expensing, and the investment credit for a car bought after June 18, 1984, you must show: (1) the car is for the convenience of your employer who requires you to use the car for your job, and (2) you used the car more than 50% for business. A letter from your employer stating you need the car for business will not meet test (1). The more than 50% test also applies to self-employed persons.

If business use is 50% or less, ACRS is barred; the auto is depreciable over a five-year period under the straight-line method subject to a mid-year convention. For 1984, this means that the first-year straight line rate is 10%, 20% in 1985, 1986, 1987, and 1988 and 10% in 1989. The straight-line method must be used in future years even though business use later exceeds 50%.

Recapture. ACRS depreciation deductions are recaptured if business use drops to 50% or less in a later year. In that year, the excess ACRS deductions over imputed straight-line deductions are reported as income. There is no recapture if straight line over a five-year period is elected.

Investment credit limitations. The investment credit for any business car may not exceed $1,000, assuming 100% business use. Further, if business use later drops to 50% or less in a later year, part of the previously claimed investment credit is reported as income. If you elect a reduced credit to avoid reduction of basis, the maximum investment credit is $670 for 100% business use.

Annual ceiling for depreciation deductions. For a car placed in service after June 18, 1984, the depreciation deduction in the first year is limited to $4,000; in the second year and third year the deduction may not exceed $6,000 each year. After the third year, the remaining basis allocated to business use may be depreciated at a rate of up to $6,000 a year until basis is written off. This rule effectively limits ACRS rates to a cost basis of up to $16,000. The $4,000 deduction ceiling also applies to the first-year expensing deduction for cars placed in service after June 18, 1984. The ceiling of $4,000 or $6,000 is applied before reducing the deduction for personal use. For example, on a car costing $40,000 but used only 90% for business, the first year ACRS deduction may not exceed $3,600 (90% of $4,000).

Mileage log to prove business use of car. Starting in 1985, a log must be kept to prove business use. The log must show the date of the trip, mileage driven, and business purpose. On your return, you will have to state that a log has been kept to substantiate your deductions. Failure to keep the log can result in penalties.

DEDUCT BUSINESS CONVENTION EXPENSES

Convention trips usually combine business with pleasure. To insure the deduction of your expenses, keep records to prove the business nature of your trip.

Be prepared to show that the convention was connected with your business. If you are a delegate to a business convention, make sure you prove that your attendance served primarily your own business interests, not those of the association. However, it is not necessary for you to show that the convention dealt specifically with your job. It is sufficient that attendance at the convention may advance or benefit your position. If you fail to prove business purpose, the IRS will allocate your expenses between the time spent on your business and the time spent as a delegate. You then deduct only the expenses attributed to your business activities. Keep a copy of the convention program and a record of the business sessions you attend. If the convention provides a sign-in book, sign it. In addition, keep a record of all of your expenses.

You may not deduct expenses at conventions held by fraternal organizations, such as the American Legion or Shriners, even though some incidental business was conducted. However, delegates to fraternal conventions may in some instances deduct their expenses as charitable contributions.

You may deduct travel costs both to and from the convention, food costs, tips, display expenses (such as sample-room costs), and hotel bills. If you entertain business clients or customers, you may deduct these amounts too.

Keep records of your payments, identifying expenses directly connected with your business dealings at the convention and those which are part of your personal activity, such as sightseeing, social visiting, and entertaining. Recreation costs are not deductible even though a part of your overall convention costs.

If your spouse accompanies you, you may deduct the cost of your spouse's participation in the entertainment of business clients at the convention. Generally, you may deduct the cost of goodwill entertaining of associates immediately before or after convention business meetings. A convention meeting qualifies as a bona fide business meeting.

If your spouse accompanies you, your bills will probably show costs for both of you. These usually are less than twice the cost for a single person. To determine how much you may deduct, do not divide the bill in half. Figure the amount it would have cost you alone for similar accommodations and transportation. Only the excess over the single person's cost is not deductible. For example, you and your spouse travel by car to a convention. You pay $40 a day for a double room. A single room would have cost $30 a day. Your spouse's presence at the convention was for social reasons. You may deduct the total cost of operating your car to and from the convention city. You may deduct $30 a day for your room. If you traveled by plane or railroad, you would deduct your fare only.

You may not deduct expenses at a foreign convention outside the North American area unless you can show that the convention was directly related to your business and it was reasonable for the meeting to be held outside the North American area.

The North American area includes Puerto Rico, U.S. possessions, the Trust Territory of the Pacific Islands, U.S. Virgin Islands, American Samoa, and Guam, Jamaica, Mexico, and Canada.

Conventions may also be held in eligible Caribbean countries which agree to exchange certain data with the U.S. and do not discriminate against conventions held in the U.S.

Up to $2,000 a year is allowed for attending cruise ship conventions if all the ports of call are in the U.S. or U.S. possessions and if the ship is registered in the United States.

HAVE AN ENTERTAINMENT ALLOWANCE ARRANGEMENT WITH YOUR COMPANY

A definite entertainment expense arrangement with your company can provide tax benefits by allowing you to claim deductions not otherwise available.

If your job requires you to incur entertainment expenses, sound tax planning requires that you and your company fix a definite policy of how the expenses will be borne. The best arrangement is for your company to give you an allowance or to reimburse you for the expenses. Try to avoid an understanding that your salary has been set to cover your payment of expenses. The following example illustrates the advantage of having a reimbursement arrangement which allows you to deduct from gross income expenses usually treated as itemized deductions.

Assume that it is understood between you and your company that your job requires paying entertainment expenses of $2,000 annually and that your net salary should be $38,000. If you are paid a straight salary of $40,000 which has to cover your payment of entertainment costs, you report $40,000 as salary income and you may deduct the $2,000 only if you itemize deductions. If you do not itemize, you may not deduct the entertainment expense. But if your salary is set at $38,000 and your company pays the entertainment costs, you report salary of $38,000 plus $2,000 for entertainment less the $2,000 for actual entertainment costs. The net amount reported on the return without the reimbursement arrangement is $40,000; with the reimbursement arrangement it is $38,000.

If you are entitled to reimbursement from your employer, make sure you receive it. Failure to be reimbursed may prevent you from deducting your out-of-pocket expenses. A supervisor whose responsibility was to maintain good relations with his district and store managers entertained them and their families and also distributed gifts among them. His cost was $2,500 for which he could have been reimbursed by his company, but he made no claim. Consequently, the court disallowed it as a deduction on his return. The expense was the company's; any goodwill he created benefited it. But because he failed to seek reimbursement, he was not allowed to convert company expenses into his own.

37

WHAT TO LOOK FOR IN A TAX SHELTER INVESTMENT

An ideal tax shelter investment should allow you to take substantial deductions in the first or early years of the investment and return income to you in later years when your tax bracket is lower.

Check how the investment provides for:

Current deductions or credits to offset or "shelter" income from other sources, such as salary, professional fees, and investment income. Substantial deductions in the early years of shelter investments may come from accelerated depreciation or unusual expenses, such as prepaid feed costs or intangible drilling costs. Similarly, a large investment credit in the first year of investment reduces taxes and returns to you part of your investment. Current write-offs also produce this bonus: the postponement of tax otherwise due on income is the equivalent of an interest-free loan from the government.

Income deferral. To recover your investment and to make a profit the plan must at some time return income, preferably in the form of capital gain. Income receipt should be deferred to later years, presumably when you will be in a lower income tax bracket.

Leveraging. Leveraging allows you to invest with minimum cash payment or up-front money, the balance being covered by borrowed funds. The opportunity of writing off expenses in excess of equity investments is barred by the "at risk" rules, which limit deductions to your risk capital in the venture, thus eliminating the tax advantages once provided by the nonrecourse financing. The investment credit is also generally limited by amounts at risk. Real estate, however, which is not covered by the "at risk" rules, may still produce substantial tax benefits through nonrecourse financing.

To assess the soundness of a prospective tax shelter venture, also check the following points:

Who are the promoters and how do they benefit? A 6%–8% commission on capital contributions is typical, but commissions can run as high as 10%. Beware of promoters who say there is no commission; there always is. Will the promoters be paid in cash, ownership interests, or both? If the promoter is your attorney or accountant, seek independent advice on the merits of the deal.

Also check on the promoters' experience in the particular type of investment, their credit rating, and whether they have conflict-of-interest problems.

Ignore promotions that boast famous persons on their list of investors. The Home Stake Oil swindle is an example of how even the rich and famous can be duped. Rely only on claims in writing; disregard a promoter's promises that are not in the prospectus.

Do not rely on the tax opinion in the prospectus. While probably correct in the academic sense, it may underplay potential problems, such as the likelihood of disputes with the IRS to establish certain tax positions.

Project the tax implications throughout the life of the venture. Be skeptical of deals offering first-year write-offs in excess of your investment; while some investments may legitimately offer first-year write-offs which exceed your cash outlay, most may not because of the "at risk" loss limitation rules. The law penalizes promoters who overstate the tax advantages of a shelter. This measure may discourage promoters from making exaggerated claims.

Is the financing sound? Proper reserves should be set up to carry loan servicing and the cost of other fixed expenses through unexpected delays or contingencies, such as acts of God, strikes, and market reverses. For instance, an otherwise well-conceived shopping mall project can fail if a strike delays construction and there are insufficient funds to pay interest on the construction loan when due.

Also, examine the manner in which the investment funds will be held until used. Are they in escrow or bank accounts? General accounts, as opposed to separate accounts for each investor, may be subject to claims by the promoter's creditor which can deplete the funds necessary to launch the venture.

What are your future financial and legal liabilities? Will you be asked to make additional investments or forfeit funds you have already contributed? Your present investment interest may be diluted if you do not make additional investments. Determine your liability for debts and tort claims. In a limited partnership, limited partners enjoy personal liability only to the extent of their investment.

What are you investing in? Is it an interest in a partnership, company, or asset, such as cattle or a box car? One tax shelter raised funds for the purpose of research and development; the investors bought only expense deductions and owed nothing. If the shelter is structured solely to produce tax benefits and lacks economic substance, deductions will be disallowed.

Can you afford to tie up your money indefinitely? While it is easy to invest in a shelter, it may be difficult to extricate your investment. Do you foresee large expenses (such as starting your own business, buying a house, or college costs for your children) for which this investment money may be needed? Some investments specify a minimum time before an investor can take his or her money out. Certain partnership interests may have restrictions on transferability.

Will the investment become a tax liability? You may be required to recognize taxable gain without receiving a payout with which to pay the tax. So-called phantom gain may arise because of tax accounting rules that require that your tax basis be reduced by certain deductions. Taxable gain may result on the foreclosure of a mortgage. The foreclosed debt is treated as sales proceeds, and although you may not receive a dollar, you are required to report a taxable gain for the difference between your tax basis and the sales proceeds allocated to your interest.

Early disposition of property on which the investment credit is claimed may also result in ordinary income in the year of recapture.

You may not avoid the phantom gain by giving away your interest. The IRS has ruled that you may not avoid phantom gain by donating your property to a charity, and a gift to a family member may also result in taxable gain if the liabilities exceed the basis of the property.

What is the likelihood of a dispute with the IRS? Your chances of being audited are increased if you claim large tax shelter losses. The IRS attempts to audit 25% of all partnerships with large losses (compared to about a 2% audit chance for the population at large). Partnership returns can alert the IRS to excessive or otherwise questionable deductions that may warrant audit of the individual partners whose names are listed with the return. For example, the IRS may challenge large deductions claimed in the first year of investment on the grounds that they result in a distortion of income.

If the tax benefits of the plan depend largely on the value of the property, the IRS may challenge that value if the investment is funded only in part by cash.

If you need a tax shelter, consider one early in the taxable year. A full write-off of certain deductions may be barred if you enter a venture late in the year. Further, last-minute haste may force you into a poor investment decision.

Under a new law, tax shelter offerings are subject to IRS registration rules. The IRS assigns to the tax shelter an identification number which each investor must list on his return when claiming tax shelter write-offs. A $50 penalty may be imposed on an investor who fails to list the number on a return unless the failure is due to reasonable cause. Promoters of registered tax shelters and any other tax shelter arrangement which the IRS considers as potentially abusive must also keep a list of investors for seven years and provide the list to the IRS upon request. Further, an investor who sells his interest in such a tax shelter to another investor must keep records identifying the buyer.

INVEST IN A REAL ESTATE TAX SHELTER

Leverage opportunities without personal liability still exist for real estate ventures with the possibility of large initial deductions and a later return of income.

A real estate venture is generally packaged as a limited partnership primarily because of tax and legal advantages offered by this partnership form which allows investors to limit their liability to the amount of their investment. Further, the limited partnership, as an organization distinct from the general and limited partners, is not taxed. Tax is imposed only on the income received by each partner. However, little or no tax may be incurred by the investors at the start of the syndicate operations because depreciation deductions are passed directly to the investors. That is, depreciation taken on the property of the syndicate reduces the partners' taxable income without reducing the amount of cash available to them. Remember, this tax saving is temporary and limited by the terms and the amount of the mortgage debt on the syndicate's property. Mortgage amortization payments reduce the amount of income available to investors without an offsetting tax deduction. Thus in the final analysis the amount of an investor's tax-free return depends on the extent to which the depreciation deductions exceed the amortization payment.

The availability of mortgage funds increases the advantage of a real estate venture; an individual may invest a limited amount of cash with the balance covered by mortgage debt. Even though investors may not be personally liable on the debt, they may claim tax deductions. However, in periods of high interest rates the amount of leverage available through mortgage financing may be limited.

Assuming the availability of adequate outside financing, a venture must obtain a constant-payment mortgage to provide a higher return of tax-free income, at least during the early years of its operations. With such a mortgage, fixed annual mortgage payments are allocated to continually decreasing amounts of interest and increasing amounts of amortization payments. Thus in the early years a tax-free return of income may be high at the same time that amortization payments are low. But as the amortization payments increase, nontaxable income will decrease. When this tax-free return has been substantially reduced, a venture must refinance the mortgage to reduce the amortization payments and once again increase the tax-free return. In states where constant-payment mortgages are difficult to secure, this tax shelter opportunity may not be available.

EXAMPLES—

1. A venture of 100 investors owns an office building that returns an annual income of $100,000 after deducting operating expenses but before deducting depreciation of $80,000. Thus taxable income is $20,000 ($100,000 less $80,000). If there is no mortgage on the building, the entire $100,000 is available for distribution. (Since the depreciation deduction requires no cash outlay, it does not reduce the cash distribution.) Each investor receives $1,000. As the venture's taxable income is $20,000, only 20% ($20,000/$100,000) of the distribution is taxable. Thus each investor reports as income only $200 of his $1,000 distribution; $800 is tax free.

2. Same facts as above, except that the building is mortgaged and an annual amortization payment of $40,000 is being made. Consequently, only $60,000 is available for distribution, of which $20,000 is taxable. Each investor receives $600, of which one-third ($20,000/$60,000), or $200, is taxed and $400 is tax free. In other words the $60,000 distribution is tax free to the same extent as the depreciation of $80,000 exceeds the amortization of $40,000—namely, $40,000. If the amortization payment was increased to $50,000, only $30,000 of the distribution would be tax free ($80,000 less $50,000).

The tax-free return is based on the assumption that the building does not actually depreciate as fast as the tax depreciation rate. Assume that an individual invests in a venture which for tax purposes is allowed to take depreciation at a rate of 5.5% a year (straight line over 18-year recovery period). If the building is actually depreciating physically at a faster rate, the so-called tax-free return does not exist. Distributions to investors (above current income return) which are labeled tax-free distributions are in fact a return of the investor's own capital.

Another advantage to consider: Sale of a building at a profit may be taxable at capital gain rates provided straight-line depreciation is elected by the venture. If not, gain may be subject to ordinary income tax rates.

Finally, none of the above advantages will result in an overall profit unless the venture has sound prospects. Therefore it is important to review the economic viability of the project. Check to see that reasonable values have been set for the property and that the projected rate of rental return is realistic, especially in the case of the purchase of a new building.

In a syndicate investment in unimproved land, the tax attraction, especially to high-bracket investors, is the opportunity to deduct the costs of carrying the property, such as interest and taxes. The deductions in turn reduce the cost of their investment with the ultimate anticipation of realizing long-term capital gain when the land is sold.

39

INVEST IN OIL AND GAS SHELTERS

Oil and gas shelters provide large initial tax deductions and the chance of a later tax shelter gain, but there are risks.

Oil and gas tax shelters involve drilling programs or royalty programs. A drilling program involves locating and drilling for oil or gas in either a "wildcat" operation or a "development" program. A wildcat operation drills for wells in unproven areas. A development operation drills for wells in producing areas.

A royalty program generally involves the purchase of interests in producing properties in exchange for future royalties. Most popular tax shelter ventures offer drilling programs packaged around a limited partnership which sells investments. To improve the chances of finding a successful well, the venture will generally drill several. If oil or gas is discovered, the partnership will either sell the rights to the well outright or operate the well and sell the oil and gas produced.

Large deductions at the start of the investment program are generated by a deduction for intangible drilling costs. Intangible drilling costs include payments for labor, fuel, and other expenses incurred in connection with drilling the well—except items which have a salvage value. Deductible intangible costs, which can be as high as 75% of an initial investment, can provide a large write-off in a year you have substantial income.

Prepayments of drilling expenses by cash-basis tax shelters are deductible in the year of payment only if drilling commences (the well is "spudded") within 90 days after the close of the year of prepayment.

Intangible drilling expenses may be recaptured as ordinary income upon the sale of the completed well. The amount of recapture is equal to the excess of the amount deducted over the amount which would have been deducted had the costs been capitalized and deducted over the life of the property as "cost depletion."

The second source of tax savings in oil and gas flows from a depletion deduction if the well begins to produce income. In most cases percentage depletion gives the larger deduction as it allows an annual deduction based on the gross income attributable to production. The amount of percentage depletion claimed is not limited by the investor's basis in the property, as in the case of cost depletion.

Percentage depletion is available only to "small producers." Small-producer status is determined at the partner level. To qualify, the partner may not engage in the retail marketing of oil or gas or gas products, and may not be a refiner of crude oil having refinery runs in excess of 50,000 barrels on any day during the taxable year. If these limitations are met, an investor may claim percentage depletion of 15% for 1984 and thereafter. This method may only be used for the first 1,000 barrels of oil or first six million cubic feet of gas produced per day.

Caution: In projecting the tax savings from an oil and gas investment, do not overlook the potential tax cost of alternative minimum tax on preference items for percentage depletion and intangible drilling costs.

Regardless of the potential tax savings, it is important to make sure that you are dealing with a reputable firm and that the investment has a reasonable chance of success. Be aware that nearly eight out of ten drilling ventures fail, and if your venture fails, you will be out of pocket despite the initial tax breaks. If it succeeds, you will have an ideal tax sheltered investment.

DETERMINING THE BREAK EVEN POINT FOR IRA INVESTMENTS

Young working people may be reluctant to invest in IRAs, believing that retirement is too far off and that they probably will need their savings over the short term for personal use. However, by investing in an IRA, a young person may be able to save more than in a regular savings account depending on how long the IRA account remains untouched.

One major tax advantage of an IRA is the tax-free accumulation of income which allows for a fast build-up of cash. However, there is a condition to this benefit. You must not withdraw the account until you reach age 59½ or become disabled. If a premature withdrawal is made, income tax plus a 10% penalty on the withdrawal may wipe out earnings in the account and also part of principal. You could recover less than if you had invested in a regular savings account.

EXAMPLE—

A person in his early twenties, and in the 30% bracket, invests $2,000 in a two-year IRA certificate earning 10% compounded daily. After two years, he needs the funds and withdraws the entire account balance of $2,443. His tax on the withdrawal is $977. This means he netted $1,466 on his $2,000 investment. This loss is attributed to the ordinary tax and penalty. If he had not invested in an IRA, he could have invested $1,400 in a regular account ($2,000 less $600 tax in the 30% bracket) at the same 10% rate. After two years, the regular account balance would be $1,617, $151 more than the IRA.

IRA account		
Balance		$2,443
Less: Tax on $2,443 at 30%	$733	
Penalty	244	977
Return after taxes		$1,466

Savings account

Balance	$1,710
Less: Tax on interest	93
Return after taxes	$1,617

An IRA is the better choice only if withdrawals are delayed until the year in which the IRA gives a greater after-tax yield than the after-tax yield of a regular investment. Take the figure of the above example but stay in the 30% tax bracket—this point is not reached until the seventh year, assuming the same tax bracket and investment return. After seven years, the IRA account will show a balance of $4,027. If it is then withdrawn, tax will be $1,611, netting $2,416. A regular savings account would show a balance of $2,819, and the net on this account would be $2,393. Here the IRA in the seventh year starts to give a greater return.

IRA account

Balance		$4,027
Less: Tax on $4,027	$1,208	
Penalty	403	1,611
Return after taxes		$2,416

Regular account

Balance		$2,819
Less: Tax on interest		426
		$2,393

The spread in favor of the IRA widens the longer the IRA is kept intact.

Note that the 10% penalty applies only to distributions before age 59½ if a disability is not shown for making the distribution. If the 10% penalty does not apply, the IRA is a better investment after one year. For example, a person 60 years of age and in the 30% bracket, by investing in an IRA, would be ahead after one year.

IRA account

Balance at end of one year	$2,210
Less: Tax on withdrawal	663
Return after taxes	$1,547

Regular account

Balance at end of year	$1,547
Less: Tax on interest	44
Return after taxes	$1,503

SELECTING LIFE INSURANCE POLICIES FOR PROTECTION AND TAX SAVINGS

To meet competition from other investment fields, life insurance companies have developed policies offering tax and investment benefits.

During the time you pay premiums, the value of your contract increases at compound interest rates. The increase is not subject to income tax. In addition, when your policy is paid at death, the proceeds are not subject to income tax. These benefits apply to almost all life insurance policies. To take advantage of these tax benefits and also to make the investment side of life insurance more attractive to investors, insurance companies have developed policies to compete with investments in the open market. Two such policies are the universal life and variable life insurance policies.

Universal life insurance plans. Universal life insurance offers tax-free build-up of interest income at current high market rates and on death, tax-free receipt of insurance proceeds. A universal life insurance policy is made up of life insurance protection and a cash reserve on which interest income accumulates without tax.

Universal life insurance differs from regular whole life in that the interest rate of universal life is pegged to current bond market rates; whole life rates are low, currently about 5%. Further, universal life lets you withdraw the cash reserve if you want to invest it elsewhere and to allocate how much of your premium payment is to cover insurance protection and how much is to go into the cash reserve.

The tax law sets limits to the amount of premiums that may be earmarked for the cash reserve. If these limits are violated, tax-free treatment for the proceeds may be lost. For these limits, check with the company issuing the policy.

You must incur an upfront commission payment which may

be 50% or more of the first premium. There may also be a fee for withdrawing the cash reserve.

Variable life insurance allows you to direct that part of your premium that should be invested in stocks and bonds. Tax on gains are deferred. Insurance coverage and cash value increase if the investments do well. If not, the policy still keeps its initial face value.

Consider variable life if you plan to keep the policy for at least 10 years. As in the case of universal life, up front fees and commissions will erode the cash value of the policy.

If you need life insurance protection and do not want to speculate with investment-pegged policies such as universal or variable life, consider term insurance. Comparatively low premium rates are available, especially by savings banks in states which allow such policies. You may tailor your own investment policy with the premium savings. However, there is this disadvantage. If you become uninsurable, you may not be able to get further life insurance protection.

SELL SAND AND GRAVEL AT LOWEST TAX COST

The way you plan a sale of sand and gravel from your land fixes tax treatment. For lowest tax cost, capital gain is preferable.

If you own land with sand or gravel deposits and you wish to turn your holding into profit, you have the choice of selling the sand or gravel or leasing the right to remove the sand or gravel. To qualify for capital gain treatment, you must sell the sand or gravel. Even if you draft the terms of the transaction as a sale, the IRS may hold that you made a lease giving the buyer only the right to extract minerals so that his payments to you are taxable as ordinary income. In disputes over the tax treatment of sales of gravel and sand, courts have developed an "economic interest" test. Under this approach, a seller who keeps an "economic interest" in the material realizes ordinary income. You are treated as having an economic interest if payments depend on extraction or production. For example, in one case a contract for the removal of sand and gravel provided for payment of a fixed amount per cubic yard of mineral removed. The contract referred to the parties as vendor and vendee. Payments were called "sales price." The seller also disclaimed retention of any economic interest in the sand and gravel. However, the payments were taxed as ordinary income. Notwithstanding the contract language, the seller retained an economic interest in the minerals. Payments were dependent on the amount of sand and gravel removed.

A provision for minimum payments not based on extraction or production may not be sufficient evidence that a sale was intended. Minimum payments are generally considered as advance royalties, taxable as ordinary income.

If a buyer is required to make payments whether or not minerals are removed, the payments may be treated as capital gain. In one case capital gain treatment was allowed where a mineral deposit was transferred in "fee simple"; the purchase price was paid at the time of the conveyance, and payment was not based on the amount of mineral extracted or set at a percentage of the mineral's retail value. The seller kept no interest in the mineral deposits and did not look to their extraction for an investment return.

PLAN AN IMPROVEMENT PROGRAM FOR RENTAL PROPERTY

If you own rental property that needs repair, make sure that you distinguish between repairs and improvements to ensure tax deductions.

Maintenance and repair expenses are not treated the same as expenses for improvements and replacements. Only maintenance and incidental repair costs are deductible from rental income. Repairs that add to the value or prolong the life of the property are capital improvements. They may not be deducted but may be added to the basis of the property and recovered through depreciation. For example, the costs of painting the outside of a building used for business purposes and the costs of papering and painting the inside are repair costs and may be deducted. The replacement of a roof or a change in the plumbing system is a capital expenditure which is added to the basis of the property.

Repairs may not be separated from capital expenditures when they are part of an improvement program. For example, you buy a dilapidated business building and have it renovated and repaired. The total cost comes to $13,000, of which $7,800 is deducted as repairs. The IRS may disallow the repair deduction because it is a capital expenditure. When a general improvement program is undertaken, you may not separate repairs from improvements. They become an integral part of overall betterment and a capital investment, although they could be characterized as repairs when viewed independently.

What if the repairs and improvements are unconnected and not part of an overall improvement program? Assume you repair the floors of one story and improve another story by cutting new windows. You may probably deduct the cost of repairing the floors, provided you have separate bills for the jobs. To safeguard the deduction, schedule the work at separate times so that the two jobs are not lumped together as an overall improvement program.

ELECT STRAIGHT-LINE DEPRECIATION FOR REAL ESTATE

Accelerated cost recovery system gives larger depreciation deductions in the first few years of the life of a building. But it may be better to spread the deductions evenly over the life of the building.

Despite the rapid write-off allowed for buildings, you may want to elect to use the straight-line method rather than the accelerated rate. The accelerated rate has tax drawbacks. Gain on a later sale is wholly or partly taxable at ordinary income rates under the recapture rules, as follows: gain on a disposition of nonresidential property is ordinary income to the extent of all accelerated recovery deductions previously allowed. Gain on a disposition of residential property is ordinary income to the extent that accelerated cost recovery deductions exceed the recovery that would have been allowed if straight-line depreciation had been elected. Election of the straight-line method avoids recapture and allows for the capital gain treatment. Further, it avoids the alternative minimum tax.

45

PLAN FOR CAPITAL GAIN ON LOT SUBDIVISIONS

If you have invested in land which has increased in value, you may want to subdivide and sell it. You must plan your activities to qualify for capital gain treatment.

Although you originally bought a tract for investment, frequent sales, advertising, listing property with agents, and making improvements increase the possibility that you may be treated as a real estate dealer by the IRS. The tax consequences of such an appraisal would subject your sales to ordinary income tax even if your main business is not real estate. You cannot avoid dealer status by hiring a realtor to develop, subdivide, or sell your property for you. The activities of an agent are imputed to an owner when carried out at his direction or with his acquiescence. To convince the IRS that you hold a piece of property as an investor, you need the following evidence to support a strong argument for capital gain:

1. You bought the property as an investment, or to use for some other personal purpose, for example, to build a residence. Or you received the property as a gift or by inheritance, or in satisfaction of a debt or claim.
2. You have held the property for a long period of time.
3. No improvements or only insubstantial ones have been added to the tract.
4. You subdivided the property to liquidate your investment because of pressure from creditors or dissension among others who hold the property with you.
5. You did not advertise or use agents. Sales came through unsolicited offers.
6. Sales were infrequent.

7. You have had no previous activities as a real estate dealer.
8. You are engaged in a profitable business unrelated to real estate. (That you have another occupation, however, does not in itself mean that you cannot also be in the real estate business.)
9. You invested the proceeds in investment property.

If you cannot meet these rules, you may still have a chance to qualify for capital gain by meeting certain statutory tests which apply to land held for at least five years. The tests put restrictions on the types of improvements that can be made and the number of sales which may be made during one taxable year.

46

A SHARED EQUITY FINANCING ARRANGEMENT MAY EASE COST OF HOME OWNERSHIP

A shared equity financing agreement is a recent approach to home ownership and financing which may provide some tax benefits.

If you are a potential homeowner, a shared equity financing arrangement may give you a chance to have someone else finance part of your home purchase. If you are an investor, it may give you a chance to make a real estate investment giving you a current return, tax deductions, and possible capital gain on future appreciation.

There are two parties to shared equity financing (1) The investor who may put up the down payment and/or contribute to the mortgage payments. In return he is paid partial rent and shares in the proceeds if the house is sold. He may deduct depreciation and currently deductible upkeep expenses paid by him; (2) The home occupant who gets the financial help to buy a home. He may deduct payment of his share of taxes and interest, build up an equity interest, and share in the future appreciation if the home is sold.

The suggested form of the deal is for both parties to buy the property as tenants-in-common, and the agreement between the parties should provide that each has a 50-year undivided interest. The 50-year requirement is set by the tax law. The occupant must use the house as his principal residence. The investor has no occupancy rights. Both share profits of the sale. The percentage is fixed by agreement of the parties. A fair rental must be paid to the investor for his ownership interest. Fair rental must take into account comparable rents in the area. If the occupant is a relative of the investor, the IRS will review whether he or she received substantial gifts from the investor.

If these tests are not met, the investor's deductions are subject to the vacation home tax law limitations.

The parties may provide for options to buy each other out after a period of time.

The occupant can be a child of the investor. This gives a parent an opportunity to help a child afford a house and to receive tax benefits. The investor can deduct ACRS depreciation on his percentage of ownership. The occupant may deduct interest and real estate taxes paid by him.

47

TIME SALES OF PROPERTY

A sale is generally taxable in the year title to the property passes to the buyer. Since you can control the year title passes, you can usually defer income realized on the sale to the year in which you will pay less tax.

Generally, a taxable transaction occurs in the year title or possession to property passes to the buyer. By controlling the year title and possession pass, you may select which year to report profit or loss. For example, you intend to sell property this year, but you estimate that reporting the sale next year will incur less tax. You can postpone the transfer of title and possession to next year. Alternatively, you can transact an installment sale, giving title and possession this year but delaying the receipt of all or most of the sale proceeds until next year.

HOW TO PROVE PROFIT MOTIVE IN VACATION HOME INVESTMENT

The high cost of carrying vacation homes can be reduced by tax deductions. But the law is designed to prevent loss deductions. To overcome these legal hurdles you must operate in a businesslike manner.

The key to securing loss deductions is proof that you made little or no personal use of the vacation residence and that you bought it to realize rental income and/or a profitable resale. The pattern of successful defenses to the IRS is set out by the following court decisions.

1. A banking executive built a ski lodge near a potential resort at Bromley Mountain in Vermont. The lodge was rented out as a summer or fall vacation home as well as during the ski season. He won his loss deductions by proving that he operated the lodge in a businesslike manner, experimenting with different types of rental arrangements in an attempt to turn a profit. He showed that substantial and repeated losses were caused by forces beyond his control—by unfavorable weather and gasoline shortages. Finally, he never used the lodge for personal enjoyment; he stayed overnight only to get the lodge in rental condition.

2. An investor bought a condominium, hired a rental agent, and even advertised the unit in newspapers. He also listed the unit for sale. In one year he was unable to rent the apartment but deducted expenses and depreciation of over $6,100 which the IRS disallowed. He won the deduction by showing that he rarely visited the apartment other than to furnish it initially. When he went on vacation, he went abroad or to other vacation spots. In later years he finally succeeded in renting the apartment.

3. An investor purchased a house and land in a coastal resort area of California. Prior to the purchase he was told by a renting agent that he could expect reasonable income and considerable appreciation from the property. After the purchase he spent $5,000 to prepare the house for rental and gave a rental

agency the exclusive right to offer the property for rent. Rentals proved disappointing, totaling only $2,000 over a two-year period, despite the active efforts of the agency to rent the property. The house appreciated in value and was eventually sold at a profit of $14,000. The investor convinced the court that the expenses of maintaining the residence were deductible, although he received minimal rent. He showed that he bought and held the property expecting to make a profit on a sale. He had previously sold similar property at a profit and so expected similar success. Finally, he rarely used it for personal purposes and an agent actively sought to rent it.

TAX OPTIONS FOR HANDLING CERTAIN COSTS OF CARRYING REAL ESTATE

If you own real estate, you have a tax-saving election for treating carrying costs.

You may elect to forgo current deductions for certain deductible taxes and other carrying charges, such as interest, in favor of capitalizing them (adding these amounts to the basis of the property). This may be to your advantage if you do not need the immediate deduction because you have little or no income to offset, do not have excess itemized deductions, or expect a great tax benefit by adding the taxes to the basis.

An election to capitalize applies not only to taxes but to interest and other deductible carrying charges incurred during your ownership of the property. To make the election, indicate your choice on your tax return. IRS permission is not required. The election, once made, may not be revoked when made for real property being improved or developed. With unimproved and nonproductive realty, the election may be made in any year, regardless of how the items were treated in a prior year.

WATCH THE TAX COST OF EXTRA EARNINGS IF YOU ARE SEMI-RETIRED

If you are semi-retired and receiving Social Security, you may find that the tax cost of extra earnings might make working in a particular year less attractive than in another year.

Part of your Social Security benefits are subject to tax if your adjusted gross income exceeds a base amount: $25,000 if you are single; $32,000 if you are married and file a joint return. If you plan to earn extra income, you should determine (1) whether the earnings will subject your benefits to tax if your income is below the base ceiling and (2) if you are under 70 years of age, whether the earnings will reduce your Social Security benefits. If you earn self-employment income, you must also figure in the cost of self-employment tax. After adding the tax on Social Security benefits and the loss of benefits, you may find that your extra earnings have netted you less than expected. In some cases, the tax increase and benefit loss may produce less spendable income than if you had not produced the extra earning.

If this is true, you may decide it does not pay to work in that particular year. If you figure that extra earnings in the next year will not bear a similar tax cost, and you are self-employed you may be able to postpone performance of the work until that year or if performance of the project is toward the end of the year, you might do the work but agree to payment in the next year.

The following is a guide to figuring the cost of extra earnings.

EXAMPLES—

1. You are over 70 and planning to work part-time. You and your spouse receive Social Security benefits of $8,000. Your adjusted gross income before adding 50% of Social Security bene-

fits is $28,000. At this point, no part of your Social Security benefits are taxable.

Adjusted gross income	$28,000
Plus: 50% of benefits	4,000
	32,000
Less: Base	32,000
No excess	0

2. Same as above except that you plan to earn up to $8,000 from a part-time job. The $8,000 will subject $4,000 of Social Security benefits to tax.

Other income	$28,000
Part-time earnings	8,000
	$36,000
50% of benefits	4,000
	$40,000
Less: Base	32,000
Excess	$ 8,000
50% of excess taxable	$ 4,000

Thus, for every dollar or extra earnings above the $32,000 or $25,000 base, fifty cents of your Social Security benefits is taxable. Here, earnings of $8,000 subject $4,000 of Social Security benefits to tax.

If you are under 70, you must also consider that Social Security benefits may be reduced by earnings from a job or self-employment.

EXAMPLE—

You are under 70, married, and your current AGI is $28,000 from investment income. Your Social Security benefit is $8,000. You are considering taking a part-time position that will pay $8,000. Assume earnings of $8,000 will reduce your Social Security benefits by $520. To determine how much you would net by working, you make the following analysis:

Without extra work:

Current AGI	$28,000
Less: Four Exemptions	
(extra 2 exemptions for age)	4,000
Taxable income	$24,000
Tax	$ 3,333

Earning extra income:

Current AGI	$28,000
Extra Earnings	8,000
Taxable Social Security benefits	4,000
	$40,000
Less: Exemptions	4,000
Taxable income	$36,000
Tax	$ 6,538

Figuring after tax income:

Earnings		$ 8,000
Less: Increase in tax		
($6,538–$3,333)	$3,205	
Loss of benefits	520	3,725
Net earnings after tax and benefit loss		$ 4,275

Further, if your earnings were subject to self-employment tax, your after-tax earnings would be further reduced.

51

KEEP INVESTMENT RECORDS AS AN ESSENTIAL PART OF ALL-AROUND TAX PLANNING

Detailed records will help you figure income and deductions at the end of the year. Do not trust your memory since you are bound to overlook items. Further, you would have no record to present to the IRS if they should call you for an audit.

You should keep a detailed record of any expense ordinary and necessary to the production of income. Keep bills for investment, legal, or tax counsel, or for rent of a safe-deposit box. Legal or accounting fees paid for advice on investments are tax deductible. Also deductible are costs involved in the preparation of a tax return.

When you hold property as an investment, keep statements of expenses pertaining to maintenance, management, or conservation of the property. You may deduct these even if there is no probability that the property ever will be sold at a gain or produce income. Included in such expenses are: (1) investment counsel fees or commissions; (2) custodian fees paid to banks or others; (3) auditors' and accountants' fees; (4) traveling costs for trips away from home to look after investments, conferring with your attorney, accountant, trustee, or investment counsel about tax or income problems; and (5) maintenance costs of idle property if effort has been made to rent or sell.

Good record keeping applies particularly to rental property because there are many deductible expenses involved. You must have a complete record of the cost of the property, including legal fees, title insurance, the date the property was acquired, the date and cost of each material alteration or addition. The records you must keep during each year include: (1) amount of rental income received; (2) bills paid for utilities and services (heat, light, water, gas, telephone, garbage); (3) bills paid for repairs (painting, cleaning, papering, redecoration); (4) property taxes; (5) management expenses; (6) salaries and wages paid to janitors, elevator operators, maintenance workers, etc., and Social Security taxes paid on their wages; (7) legal expense for drawing leases, dispossessing tenants, or acquiring tenants; (8) fire, liability, plate-glass insurance premiums; and (9) interest on mortgage or other indebtedness.

That you rent only one-half of your house, or one room out of eight, does not change the need for a record of every item. In renting part of your house you may deduct a proportionate part of the expense of running the house against the rental income. You will not know how much to deduct unless you have a record of all expenses. On the same statement, keep an explanation of the basis of the apportionment you use for the tax return.

For dividend and interest income from stocks and bonds or for trading investments, keep a record of: (1) name of issuing company; (2) number of shares or bonds owned and certificate or serial number of each; (3) date of purchase; (4) amount paid (including stamp taxes and broker's fees); (5) date of sale; (6) amount received (net after stamp taxes and broker's fees); (7) broker's statements; and (8) each dividend or interest payment received.

Your records should be kept for a minimum of three years after the year to which they apply. Some authorities advise keeping them for six years, since in some cases the IRS may go back as far as six years to question a tax return. In cases of suspected tax fraud there is no time limitation.

Also keep copies of information returns sent to you and the IRS by your employer, payers of interest and dividend income, and sale of securities. Check that the data agree with your record of income. If the IRS finds any discrepancy between what is reported on the information return and your tax return, you may be subject to an audit. If the payor has made an error, have the payer prepare a corrected form.

Brokers are now required to report to the IRS the proceeds from sales of stocks, bonds and commodities transacted by their customers. The information, listed on Form 1099-B is used by the IRS to check the reporting of the sales on individual tax returns.

Exchange-traded stock options are not currently subject to broker reporting.

52

MAKE YEAR-END SALES TO REDUCE YOUR TAXES

During the year you may have sold stocks, bonds, and other property for profit or loss. Before the year is out you may want to make further sales for tax advantage.

To plan your year-end tax-saving strategy, find your gain and loss position for the year. Then study how to reduce your tax liability or improve your investment position. Review records of earlier years for capital losses which may be applied against your current gains. Include nonbusiness bad debts as short-term capital losses. After listing gains and losses realized during the year, review them to determine transactions that might now be completed to—

Offset actual gains
Utilize potential losses
Step up the tax cost of your securities
Improve your tax position for future years

The following checklist provides suggestions for deciding which securities or other property to sell.

If your completed transactions show:

Long-term gain. You might avoid taking any losses this year and pay tax on these gains at capital gain rates. If you want to realize losses, sell property held long term for long-term losses.

Short-term gain. You might realize losses to offset these gains. Sell property held long term to offset these gains.

Long-term loss. You might consider realizing gains that would be offset by these losses. Sell property giving short-term gain to take advantage of the full amount of the loss. Net long-term capital losses in excess of short-term capital gain are subject to this limitation: only 50% of the net long-term loss is deductible from up to $3,000 of ordinary income. Therefore to take advantage of the full loss it is advisable to realize short-term gains. For instance, if you do not have short-term gains, you might consider selling a stock having a paper long-term gain with an immediate repurchase of the stock. The gain is offset by the loss; on the repurchase, your tax basis is increased.

Short-term loss. You might consider realizing short-term gains to offset these losses. In planning the extent of your sales, note that short-term losses up to $3,000 may be deducted in full from ordinary income.

Net short-term gain and net long-term gain. You might sell property giving short-term loss not in excess of the short-term gain.

Net long-term gain and net short-term loss. You might sell property giving short-term gain up to the amount of short-term loss.

Net short-term gain and net long-term loss. If the long-term loss is equal to the short-term gain, you might consider no further transactions as the loss eliminates the gain. If net short-term gain exceeds the net long-term loss, you might sell securities to realize long-term loss to the extent of the excess. If the net long-term loss exceeds the net short-term gain, you might sell securities to realize short-term gain up to the extent of the excess loss.

Remember, these guides consider only the tax consequences. You must also weigh the investment value of your stock or other property and general market and economic conditions. If you are interested in a stock because of its long-term potential, you might delay buying until late in December or perhaps in January of the following year for possible price decline due to year-end selling.

Realizing losses may pose a problem if you believe the stock is due to increase in value sometime in the near future. The wash sale rule prevents you from taking the loss if you buy 30 days before or after the sale.

Postponing taxable gain on securities sales. If you do not want to realize taxable gains on a security this year, but you think that the price of your stock may decline by the time you make the sale next year, you can freeze your profit by ordering a short sale of the stock in this year. You transact a short sale by selling shares borrowed from your broker. In January of next year you deliver the shares to your broker as a replacement of the borrowed shares you sold this year. By delivering the stock next year, the gain on the short sale is fixed for next year. For tax purposes a short sale is not completed until the covering stock is delivered.

In planning year-end sales, watch the deadline for recording stock market sales. The deadline depends on whether you have a gain or loss and are on the cash or accrual basis. When you buy and sell securities through a registered stock exchange, the holding period starts on the day after the "trade date," although you do not pay for and receive the securities until several days later on the "settlement date." Similarly, the holding period ends on the day you sell the securities (the "trade date") even though you do not deliver or receive payments for the securities until the later "settlement date." The reason for the intervening days is that stock exchanges do not require delivery and payment until the third or fourth full business day after the day on which a sale or purchase is ordered. Often the period may be longer because of intervening holidays.

Although this stock exchange practice does not affect the tax consequences of security transactions made during the year, it may affect the timing of gain taken at the end of the year. Because of the holiday season, the settlement date of a sale ordered a week before the end of the year may occur in the next year, with this result: a gain which you wanted to report as income this year is taxable next year. The reason: As a cash basis taxpayer, you do not realize gain until you actually or constructively receive payment, that is, on the "settlement date." However, under installment reporting rules you may elect to report your gain this year. For example, a sale ordered at the end of December 1985, for which payment is received at the beginning of January 1986, is considered an installment sale. Thus you have an opportunity to "elect out" of installment reporting by reporting the gain in the year of sale, 1985, rather than in 1986 when payment is received. The decision to elect out of installment reporting may be made as late as the time for filing your return (plus extensions). Thus if you make a year-end sale, you have several months to decide in which year to report the sale.

If you are selling at a loss, you can do so until the last business day of the year, regardless of the settlement dates. If you are on the accrual basis, you have until the last business day of the year to realize both gains and losses.

53

GOOD STOCK RECORDS CAN PAY OFF

Keep a record of all your stock transactions, especially when you buy the stock of one company at varying prices. A record of each stock lot may allow you to control the amount of gain or loss on a sale of a part of your holdings.

Good record keeping can be turned into a tax advantage. Assume that over a three-year period you bought the following shares of Deep Well Oil stock: in 1976, 100 shares at $77 per share; in 1977, 200 shares at $84 per share; in 1979, 100 shares at $105 per share. When the stock is selling at $90 you plan to sell 100 shares. You may use the cost of your 1979 lot and claim a $1,500 loss if, for example, you want to offset some gains or other income you have already earned this year. Or you may qualify for capital gains of varying amounts by either selling the 1976 lot or part of the 1977 lot. You must clearly identify the lot you want to sell. Assume you want a loss and sell the 1979 lot. Unless you identify it as the lot sold, the IRS will hold that you sold the 1976 lot under the "first-in, first-out" rule. This rule assumes that when you have a number of identical items bought at different times, your sale of any of them is automatically the sale of the first you bought. So the cost of your first purchase is matched against your selling price to determine your gain or loss. However, if you do not want the first-in, first-out rule to apply, you must show that you delivered the 1979 stock certificates which were registered in your name.

If your stock is held by your broker, the IRS considers that an adequate identification is made if you grant him or her the power to buy and sell in your name at will. Your broker must notify you at the time of sale, requesting instructions on which shares to sell. Before the settlement date (usually four business days from the time of sale), you instruct your broker by letter which shares to deliver. He or she in turn signs and dates the confirmation, which is printed at the bottom of your letter of instruction, and returns the letter to you. In addition your broker submits to you monthly statements of the transactions and your cash position and stock on hand.

If you need a further incentive to keep your record straight, consider what happened to a group of New Jersey investors who failed to keep adequate records of thousands of stock certificates they bought and sold. When they did sell, they were unable to prove which certificates were delivered for sale. Enter the Internal Revenue Service. Upon discovering that the records were inadequate, it recomputed the sales as though the first shares bought by the investors were the first lot sold. As a result, the group was hit with a tax deficiency of $600,000.

54

USE EXCHANGES TO IMPROVE YOUR INVESTMENT WITHOUT TAX

Take advantage of tax-free exchange rules to defer the tax on gain while upgrading your investment portfolio.

You may own investment property, such as a piece of land, which has appreciated considerably. If you sell for cash, you will have to pay tax on your profit. However, if you can find another parcel of land equal in value to your land and you and the other landholder exchange lots, you have improved your property holding but you are not required to pay tax currently. Gain may be taxed at a later disposition of the property because the basis of the property received in the exchange is determined by the property surrendered. Thus, if you make a tax-free exchange, giving up property with a tax basis of $10,000 for property worth $50,000, the basis of the property received in exchange is $10,000, even though its fair market value is $50,000. The gain of $40,000 ($50,000 less $10,000) is not recognized. If you later sell the property for $50,000, you realize taxable gain of $40,000 ($50,000 less $10,000).

If property received in a tax-free exchange is held until death, the nonrecognized gain escapes tax forever because the heir generally takes as his basis the value of the property at death.

The property traded must be solely for property of a like kind. The words "like kind" are liberally interpreted, referring to the nature or character of the property, not its grade, quality, or use. For example, an exchange of gold for gold coins or silver for silver coins may qualify as a tax-free exchange of like-kind property. An exchange is tax free if both coins represent the same type of underlying investment. An exchange of bullion-type coins for bullion-type coins is a tax-free like-kind exchange. For example, the exchange of Mexican pesos for Austrian coronas has been held to be a tax-free exchange as both are bullion-type coins. On the other hand an exchange of U.S. gold collector's coins for South African Krugerrands is taxable. Krugerrands are bullion-type coins whose value is determined solely by metal content, whereas the U.S. gold coins are numismatic coins whose value depends on age, condition, number minted, and artistic merit, as well as metal content. Although both coins appear to be similar because of gold content, they each represent different types of investments. The IRS has also ruled that silver and gold bullion are not like kind; silver is an industrial commodity whereas gold is primarily an investment in itself.

Time limits for deferred exchanges. One of the parties to an exchange may not have at the time of contract property which he has promised to exchange. Under prior law, a delay in closing the exchange was not fatal to tax-free treatment. Under a new law, the exchange must generally be completed within a 180-day period. The qualifying period may even be shorter than 180 days. Property will *not* be treated as like-kind property if received after (1) 180 days after the date you relinquished property, or (2) the due date of your return for the year in which you made the transfer, whichever date is earlier. If the due date falls within a period of less than 180 days, ask for an extension to file your return.

The property to be received must also be identified within 45 days after the date on which you transferred property. The 45-day test may be met by describing the property in the contract or by listing a limited number of properties that may be transferred, provided the particular property to be transferred depends on contingencies beyond the control of both parties. For example, you transfer real estate for Smith's promise to transfer property X if zoning changes are approved or property Z if they are not. The exchange will qualify provided the contract covers these points and is made within the time limit.

55

AVOID THE WASH SALE RULE

You may want to convert paper losses into real losses to off-set gains while maintaining your investment position in the security. The wash sale rules prevent you from qualifying for a loss deduction if you sell the security and then re-cover your position within a short period of time.

The penalty period covers 61 days: 30 days before and 30 days after the date of the sale of securities. The penalty applies also if you sell at a loss and your spouse buys the securities. For example, you cannot deduct a loss from the sale of stock on Monday if you buy additional shares of the same stock on Tuesday.

How can you avoid the rule? You can, of course, delay your purchase until after the 30-day period if you feel that the value of the security will not increase within that time. If you are dealing with bonds of the same obligor, you may have greater flexibility in selling a bond at a loss and immediately recovering your position in bonds of the same company with different interest rates. You must avoid buying bonds of the same obligor that are considered substantially identical, that is, if they carry the same rate of interest; different issue dates and interest payment dates will not remove them from the wash sale provisions. Different maturity dates will have no effect unless the difference is economically significant. If there is a long span of time between the purchase date and the maturity date, a difference of several years between maturity dates may be considered insignificant. A difference of three years between maturity dates was held to be insignificant when the maturity dates of the bonds, measured from the time of purchase, were 45 and 48 years away. There was no significant difference when the maturity dates differed by less than one year and the remaining life, measured from the time of purchase, was more than 15 years.

A warrant falls within the wash sale rule if it is an option to buy substantially identical stock. Consequently, a loss on the sale of common stocks of a corporation is disallowed when warrants for common of the same corporation are bought within the period 30 days before or after the sale. But if the timing is reversed, that is, you sell warrants at a loss and simultaneously buy common of the same corporation, the wash-sale rules may or may not apply, depending on whether the warrants are substantially identical to the purchased stock. This is determined by comparing the relative values of the stock and warrants. The wash sale rule will apply only if the relative values and price changes are similar enough to make the warrants fully convertible securities.

Sometimes the wash sale rule can work to your advantage. Assume that during December you are negotiating a sale that will bring you a large capital gain. You want to offset part of that gain by selling certain securities at a loss. You are unsure when the gain transaction will go through. It may be on the last day of the year. If so, it may be too late to sell the loss securities before the end of the year. You can protect your position by selling the loss securities during the last week of December. If the profitable deal goes through before the end of the year, you need not do anything further. If it does not, buy back the loss securities early in January. The December sale will be a wash sale and the loss disallowed. When the profitable sale occurs next year, you can sell the loss securities again. This time the loss will be allowed and will offset the gain.

Wash sale rules apply also to short sales.

TAX-SAVING OPTIONS OF U.S. SAVINGS BONDS

U.S. Series EE Savings Bonds provide tax options not available in other investments.

U.S. Savings Bonds (EE) may be cashed in for their purchase price plus an increase in their value. The increase over cost is taxed as interest. You do not have to report the annual increase in value. If you choose, you may defer the interest income until the year you cash in the bond or the year the bond finally matures, whichever is earlier. Alternatively, you may elect this year to report annual increases and report the total of increases in value in prior years. Next year you report only the increases accruing then, plus increases accruing in newly purchased bonds. Once you make the election, you must continue reporting annual increases unless you obtain IRS permission to change your method of reporting.

Which option should you elect? If you are now in a high tax bracket, it is usually advisable to defer interest reporting because you may be in a lower tax bracket when the interest is taxable. Further, you save the amount that would be used to pay current taxes. However, if you bought bonds in your children's names as an investment for college, you may save taxes by having the child report the interest annually on his or her return. The child may pay little or no tax on the interest. Reporting the interest annually will usually be the better alternative because, if taxes are deferred, the child will have to pay tax on the accumulated interest when the bonds are redeemed to pay college costs, reducing the amount available for expenses.

INVEST FOR TAX-EXEMPT INCOME

Interest rates on tax-exempt bonds are generally lower than those of corporate bonds or Treasury bills and bonds of comparable safety and quality. However, if you are in a high tax bracket, the difference in interest rates may be more than offset by the tax that would be incurred on the higher interest.

To compare the interest return of a tax-exempt with that of a taxable bond, figure the taxable return that is equivalent to the tax-free yield of the tax exempt. This amount depends on your tax bracket. For example, for a person whose income is subject to a top tax rate of 50%, a municipal bond yielding 9% is the equivalent of a taxable yield of 18%. The following table shows the amount a taxable bond would have to earn to equal the tax-exempt bond, according to the investor's income tax bracket.

| If top income tax rate is: | *A tax-exempt yield of | | | | | | | |
| | 9% | 10% | 11% | 12% | 13% | 14% | 15% | 16% |
	is the equivalent of these taxable yields:							
29%	12.7	14.1	15.5	16.9	18.3	19.7	21.1	22.5
33%	13.4	14.9	16.4	17.9	19.4	20.9	22.4	23.9
39%	14.8	16.4	18.0	19.7	21.3	23.0	24.6	26.2
44%	16.1	17.9	19.6	21.4	23.2	25.0	26.8	28.6
49%	17.6	19.6	21.6	23.5	25.5	27.5	29.4	31.4
50%	18.0	20.0	22.0	24.0	26.0	28.0	30.0	32.0

* Exemption from the tax of the state issuing the bond will increase the yield.

To lock in high rates, you may have to invest in a long-term bond. However, consider these drawbacks: You may not want to tie up your capital long term. There is the possibility that a future increase in interest rates may reduce the value of your investment if you should need the principal before maturity.

There are capital gain opportunities in tax-exempts which are selling at a discount because they pay interest at rates lower than current rates. Bonds bought at discounts can yield capital gains if held to maturity. Assume you have $25,000 to invest. You have a choice of bonds which will mature in 14 years, one a par bond selling at 100 and one a discount bond selling at 62.12. Here is a comparison of returns if you are in the 50% tax bracket:

	Discount bond	Par bond
Interest rate	5.7%	12%
Principal of bonds	$40,000	$25,000
Amount of investment	$24,848	$25,000
Annual tax-free interest	$ 2,280	$ 3,000
Total interest to maturity	$31,920	$42,000
Capital gains after tax	$12,122	0
Total after-tax return	$44,042	$42,000

The new tax rule subjecting market discount to ordinary income tax does not apply to tax-exempt obligations.

Most municipal bonds issued before July 1, 1983 except for housing issues are in the form of bearer bonds; the owners are not identified and interest coupons are cashed as they come due. However, state and municipal bonds issued after June 30, 1983 with a maturity of more than one year, as well as obligations of the federal government and its agencies, are in registered form. Principal and interest is transferable only through an entry on the books of the issuer. The Treasury plans a system for registering obligations now held in street name.

TAX OPTIONS IN TREATING BOND PREMIUMS

Bond premium is the extra amount paid for a bond in excess of its par value. You may elect to amortize bond premium or leave the basis of the bond unchanged. Amortizing is usually advisable.

If you do not amortize the premium, you will realize a capital loss when the bond is redeemed at par or you sell it for less than you paid for it. For example, you buy a $1,000 corporate bond for $1,150. You do not amortize the premium of $150. When the bond is redeemed at par, you will realize a long-term loss of $150. The premium is treated as part of the basis of the bond.

Redemption proceeds	$1,000
Cost basis	1,150
Loss	($150)

Why is amortizing the premium annually usually the advisable method? You get a current deduction against ordinary income if you claim excess itemized deductions. You also reduce the cost basis of the bond by the amount of the premium taken as a deduction. If you hold the bond to maturity, the entire premium is amortized and you have neither gain nor loss on redemption of the bond. If you sell the bond at a gain (selling price exceeds your basis for the bond), you realize long-term capital gain if you hold the bond long term. A sale of the bond for less than its adjusted basis gives a capital loss.

If you choose to amortize, the election applies to all bonds owned by you at the beginning of the first year you make the choice and to all bonds acquired thereafter. You make an election to amortize by taking the deduction on your tax return in the first year you decide to amortize the bond premium. If you file your return without claiming the deduction, you may not change your mind and make the election by filing an amended return or refund claim.

Premium paid on bonds with original issue discount. The premium may be amortized on the straight-line method over the remaining term of the bond bought on or before July 18, 1984. For bonds bought after July 18, 1984, the premium is amortized by reducing original issue discount by a fraction. The numerator of the fraction is the premium; the denominator is the amount of the original issue discount still remaining on the bond at the time of purchase.

NOTE: You may not take a deduction for the amortization of premium paid on a tax-exempt bond. When you dispose of the bond, you amortize the premium for the period you held the bond and reduce the basis of the bond by the amortized amount.

INVEST IN UTILITIES OFFERING TAX-FREE STOCK DIVIDENDS

There is a special incentive to invest in certain public utilities. If the utility qualifies, dividends which are taken in stock rather than cash are tax free up to $750, up to $1500 on joint returns.

Only certain public utilities may offer these special tax-free dividend plans. Your broker should have a list of companies that qualify. If you elect to take your dividend from a qualifying utility in the form of common stock, you may exclude up to $750 ($1,500 on joint returns) of stock received each year from 1982 through 1985. Dividends received after 1985 will not qualify for the exclusion unless the law is extended.

You may not claim the exclusion if you own, either directly or indirectly through related parties, more than 5% of the utility's stock or voting power.

When you sell the stock received as a dividend, the entire proceeds are taxable because your cost basis in the stock is considered to be zero. If the stock is worth $500 when sold, you must report the entire $500 as profit. However, your profit will be taxed at favorable long-term capital gain rates if these tests are satisfied: (1) you hold the dividend shares for more than one year, and (2) you do not sell any other common stock of the utility during the period beginning with the record date of the dividend and ending one year after the date the dividend is distributed.

If other stock is sold within the one-year period described in test 2, you will be treated as if you had sold the dividend stock (test 1). Proceeds attributable to the number of your dividend shares will be taxed as ordinary income. The remaining proceeds will qualify as long-term capital gain.

If you are receiving Social Security benefits, consider this investment as a means of improving investment holdings without affecting the tax, if any, on Social Security benefits. While the receipt of exempt interest income may subject part of your Social Security benefits to tax after 1983, excluded dividend income does not.

WHEN TO DEFER INCOME AND ACCELERATE DEDUCTIONS

When you expect to pay less tax in a future year than in a current year, you may consider deferring income and accelerating deductions.

There are two strategies to follow to maximize tax savings if you expect to pay less tax in a later year: postpone the receipt of income to a year of lower tax rates, and/or claim deductions for losses and expenses in the year you are subject to higher rates.

In planning to defer income and accelerate deductions, you must be aware of these tax rule limitations. You may not defer salary income by not cashing a paycheck or not taking salary which you have earned and which you can receive without restrictions. Under certain conditions you may contract with your employer to defer the taxable receipt of current compensation to future years. To defer pay to a future period, you must take some risk. You cannot have any control over your deferred pay account. If you are not confident of your employer's ability to pay in the future, you should not defer pay.

If you are self-employed and are on the cash basis, you can defer income by delaying your billing at the end of the year or extending the time of collection. If you own a closely held corporation, you can time the payment of dividends and bonuses.

In accelerating deductions, there are these limitations. You may not deduct prepaid interest and rent. Prepaid interest must be deducted over the period of the loan. Rentals must also be deducted over the rental period. However, you can generally deduct prepayments of state income tax and accelerate your payments of charitable contributions. Subscriptions to professional journals and business magazines can be renewed before the end of the year. If you are considering the purchase of a car or boat, do so before the end of the year to increase the amount of your sales tax deduction. Contributions, purchases, and expenses charged to a credit card account are deductible in the year of charge even though you do not pay your charge-account bill until the next year. You can also realize losses by selling property which has lost value in the year you want to incur the loss.

DEFER INTEREST INCOME TO NEXT YEAR

Buying six-month certificates after June 20 can defer interest reporting to next year.

As a general rule, you have to report interest credited to your savings account for 1985, even though you do not present your passbook to have the amount entered. Similarly, interest coupons due and payable in 1985 are taxable on your 1985 return regardless of when they were presented for collection. For example, a coupon due in December 1985 but presented for payment in 1986 is taxable in 1985. However, there are opportunities to defer interest in the following ways.

1. Buy a six-month certificate after June 30. Interest is taxable in the next year when the certificate matures unless you receive interest during the year. Your bank may offer you the choice of when to receive the interest.

2. Buy Treasury bills which come due next year. Six-month bills bought after June 30 will mature in the next year. You can make these purchases through your bank or broker.

3. Buy Series EE bonds. These bonds may be cashed for their purchase price, plus an increase in their value over stated periods of time. The increase in redemption value is taxed as interest. You do not have to report the annual increase in value. You may defer the interest income until the year you cash the bond or the year the bond finally matures, whichever is earlier.

HOW TO MAXIMIZE SALES TAX DEDUCTIONS

State and local sales taxes are deductible. Estimating the deduction from the IRS tables may not give you the maximum deduction.

You may use the IRS sales tax table to make your estimate. The table is in the instruction booklet accompanying your return. As helpful as the table may be to many persons, you may find it inadequate. The IRS estimate does not include purchases of expensive items, such as autos, boats, airplanes, mobile homes, and materials used to build a new home if you are your own contractor. If you bought such an item, you should add the sales tax paid to the amount listed in the table, provided the tax rate was the same as the general tax rate and the tax was stated separately from the sales price. You may not add the sales tax on purchases of any other large and unusual items, such as furniture and appliances. The IRS position is arbitrary, but as the table is an administrative measure, the IRS has the authority to fix the rules for its use. In this, the IRS has court support. One court has not allowed deductions for sales taxes paid on furniture in addition to the amounts allowed by the table.

The IRS table may also not reflect your rate of spending. There is only one alternative: keep a record of all expenditures. Put all your receipts in an envelope and total the tax at the end of the year. It is a chore, but the extra deduction may be worth the time. Further, if a deduction is questioned, the bulk of the receipts and tape records should help convince an agent of your deduction.

In general, you may deduct general sales taxes imposed on you as the consumer of the property or services. Those levied upon the retailer are deductible by you as the consumer if they are collected or charged as separate items.

Retail sales taxes on motor vehicles are deductible. However, if the rate charged on the car exceeds the general sales tax rate, you may deduct only that part of the tax that would have been charged at the lower general sales tax rate.

Sales taxes on materials in home construction are generally deductible if you acted as your own contractor and purchased and paid for the materials. However, when you contract with a builder to construct the house at a fixed price or on a cost-plus basis, you may not claim sales tax deduction for materials he buys. He is considered the purchaser, although the sales tax the builder pays on materials is reflected in the price and is passed on to you.

Do not overlook deducting compensating use tax you may have paid on the purchase of a car out of stock. A compensating use tax is generally imposed on the use or consumption of an item brought in from another taxing jurisdiction. A use tax is deductible if imposed at the same rate as the general sales tax and if complementary to a general sales tax which is also deductible under the above rules.

AVOIDING THE IMPACT OF THE ALTERNATIVE MINIMUM TAX

You will lose the tax benefits of tax shelter plans if you fall within alternative minimum tax. Advance planning can avoid or soften the effect of the tax.

The alternative minimum tax (AMT) is designed to recoup tax benefits which have reduced or eliminated your regular income tax. AMT is imposed if it exceeds your regular income tax or you have no tax liability after claiming certain tax deductions called "preference items," or credits. You may incur an AMT if you have—

> Substantial long-term capital gains which are your major or only source of income
> Deductions for accelerated and ACRS depreciation, percentage depletion, and intangible drilling and development costs, and/or
> A substantial investment credit.

Even when you do not have the above preference items, you may incur an AMT if you have substantial itemized deductions that are not deductible for AMT purposes. For AMT purposes, state and local income taxes are not deductible and there is a limited interest deduction.

The AMT rate is 20% after deducting an exemption of $30,000 if you are single ($40,000 if married and filing jointly).

If you expect to reduce substantially your regular tax through tax shelter benefits, make sure to project your possible AMT liability. This may involve complicated calculations and it may be advisable to have an experienced accountant help you. If you are close to or within the range of the AMT tax, the following steps can avoid or soften the impact of the tax.

> Defer the realization of long-term capital gains to a later year. You can defer gains by transacting an installment sale or if you are selling securities you

can transact short sales. You may also reduce capital gains by realizing capital losses.

Defer deductible expense items to a later year in which your income will be subject to tax rates exceeding 20%. Consider deferring payment of taxes, charitable donations, interest, and medical expenses. In deferring real estate taxes, consider the effect of penalties or tax liens. You will get a larger tax benefit from the deductions in the later year. In the case of certain realty or equipment purchases, consider an election to capitalize taxes and carrying charges. You might consider adding the sales tax to the cost basis of a business car rather than claiming the tax as a deduction. Also, do not elect first-year expensing of business equipment.

Defer the payment of state and local taxes. If you are subject to AMT tax, state and local taxes are not deductible for AMT purposes.

Defer if possible the exercise of an incentive stock option to a later year. The bargain element of incentive stock option is a preference item subject to AMT. This is the difference between the option price and the fair market price of the stock on the date of exercise. If you exercise the option and it is subject to AMT along with other tax shelter preferences, you may find yourself with an unexpected liability and short of liquid funds to meet your tax liability.

Accelerating ordinary income. If you find that you will be subject to AMT in a current year, consider accelerating the receipt of ordinary income to that year. If you are in business, you might ask for earlier payments from customers or clients. If you control a small corporation, you might prepay salary or pay larger bonuses. But here be careful not to run afoul of reasonable compensation rules. You might also consider paying dividends. If you hold savings certificates with a six-month maturity in a later year, you might consider an early redemption to the current year. But here weigh the cost of an interest forfeiture. Similarly you might make an early sale of U.S. Treasury Bills to the current year. You may also consider realizing short-term capital gains if they will be subject to 20% AMT rate.

If you are certain that you will be subject to AMT you may consider switching some tax-free investments into taxable investments which will give a higher after-tax return after the 20% AMT tax.

HOW TO SUPPORT YOUR CASUALTY LOSS DEDUCTION

Substantial casualty loss deductions may attract IRS review. If your return is audited, you will have to prove that the casualty occurred and also prove the amount of the loss. The time to collect your evidence is as soon after the casualty as possible, not when your return is audited.

You must prove that a casualty actually occurred. With a well-known casualty, like regional floods, you have no difficulty proving the casualty occurred, but you must still prove it affected your property. Before and after photographs of the area, newspaper stories, and pictures placing the damage in your neighborhood are helpful.

If only your property has been damaged, you may take photographs to use as evidence. There might be a newspaper item on the event. Some papers list all the fire alarms answered the previous day. Police, fire, and other municipal departments may have reports on the casualty.

Appraisals by a competent expert are important and should be in writing in the form of an affidavit, deposition, estimate, or appraisal. The expert, whether an appraiser, engineer, or architect, should be qualified to judge local values. If you have any records of offers to buy your property, either before or after the casualty, they can also help. The Kelley Blue Book may be used as a guide in fixing the value of a car. But an amount offered for your car as a trade-in on a new car is not usually accepted as a measure of value.

Cost of repairs is allowed as a measure of loss of value if it is not excessive and does nothing more than restore your property to its condition immediately before the casualty. Collect canceled checks, bills, receipts, and vouchers for expenses of clearing debris and restoring the property to its condition before the casualty. If the repairs will not be made until the following year, obtain bills or estimates. You deduct the loss in the year of the casualty, not when you pay the expenses.

A deed, contract, bill of sale, or other document probably shows your original cost. You should also have bills, receipts, canceled checks, etc., to show the cost of any improvements since you acquired the property. Courts usually require strict proof of cost basis. One court refused to allow a deduction because an owner failed to prove the original cost of a destroyed house and its value before the fire. In another case estimates were allowed where a fire destroyed records of cost. A court held that the homeowner could not be expected to prove cost by documents lost in the fire that destroyed her property. She made inventories after the fire and again at a later date. Her reliance on memory to establish cost, even though inflated, was no bar to the deduction. The court estimated the market values based on her inventories.

If you did not buy your property but acquired it by gift or inheritance, you must establish your adjusted basis in the property from records of the donor or the executor of the estate.

WHEN TO CLAIM DISASTER LOSSES

The law allows a tax break if you suffer uninsured property damage in a flood, hurricane, or other disaster which is declared eligible for federal assistance. You may choose whether to deduct your loss on the tax return for the year of the disaster, or the return for the year before the disaster.

Every year storms and floods hit certain localities so hard that the President declares them disaster areas eligible for federal assistance. If your property is damaged in such a disaster, you have the option of when to deduct your loss. If the disaster occurs before April 15, you may deduct the loss on the tax return for the prior year if you have not yet filed that return. For example, if your loss occurs in February 1985, you may deduct the loss on your 1984 return filed by April 15, 1985. This may allow you to receive an immediate cash refund on your 1984 return, or at least reduce the taxes due, instead of having to wait until April 15, 1986, to deduct the loss on your 1985 return. Only losses in excess of 10% of your adjusted gross income are deductible.

Claiming the deduction for the year before the year of the disaster may not always pay. Using the above example, you might anticipate that your tax bracket will be higher in 1985 than in 1984. If so, by waiting and taking the deduction in 1985 you would save more in taxes. However, the greater tax savings by delaying the deduction might be less important than the immediate 1984 deduction if it is needed to provide cash.

You also have these options: (1) If you do not claim the deduction on the prior year's return, you have until the due date for the year of the disaster to change your mind. That is, you have until April 15, 1986, to either claim the deduction on your 1985 return or amend your previously filed 1984 return and claim the disaster loss then if that would provide the greatest tax savings. (2) If you deducted the loss on the return for the year before the disaster (the 1984 return in our example) you could still change your mind until the due date for your 1985 return, or April 15, 1986. You may revoke the earlier deduction and instead claim the deduction in the year of the loss.

Under a new law, homeowners forced to relocate or demolish homes in a federally declared disaster area may deduct losses attributable to the disaster without having to prove that a sudden "casualty" has occurred. For example, because of progressive erosion, there may be a danger of flooding to certain beachfront homes which results in a government order to relocate the residence. Under prior law, damage due to progressive erosion could not be deducted as a casualty. Under the new law, a loss is treated as resulting from a casualty and a deduction is allowed if these tests are met: (1) The President has determined that the area warrants Federal disaster relief; (2) within 120 days of the President's order, the homeowner is ordered by the state or local government to demolish or relocate the residence, and (3) the home was rendered unsafe by the erosion or other disaster. The law applies to any residence, not merely to principal residences.

The loss is treated as a disaster loss so that the homeowner may elect to deduct the loss either in the year the demolition or relocation order is made or in the prior taxable year.

The new disaster loss rule applies in taxable years ending after 1981 to residences in areas declared to be disaster areas after 1981 by the President. Individuals who qualify under the new law may file a refund claim. If demolition or relocation was ordered in 1982, a refund claim may be made for 1982 or 1981. If the order was in 1983, the deduction is allowed only to the extent it exceeds 10% of adjusted gross income; the 10% floor also applies if the election is made to deduct the loss for the prior 1982 year.

HOW TO QUALIFY FOR FOREIGN TAX-FREE INCOME

You can earn up to $80,000 tax free by working abroad.

Working and living abroad does not relieve you of your obligation to file and pay U.S. income tax. However, due to the foreign earned income exclusion you may not owe any tax. To claim the exclusion for foreign income, you must meet the foreign residency test or a physical presence test in a foreign country. You must be a bona fide resident of a foreign country for an uninterrupted period that includes one full tax year. If you are abroad more than one year but less than two, the entire period qualifies if it includes one full tax year.

To prove you are a foreign resident, you must show your intention to be a resident of the foreign country. Evidence confirming your intention to stay in a foreign country is: your family accompanies you; you buy a house or rent an apartment rather than a hotel room; you participate in the foreign community activities; you speak the foreign language; you have a permanent foreign address; you join clubs there; or you open charge accounts in stores in the foreign country.

You will not qualify if you take inconsistent positions toward your foreign residence. You will not be treated as a bona fide resident of a foreign country if you have earned income from sources within that country, filed a statement with the authorities of that country that you are not a resident there, and have been held not subject to the income tax of that country. However, this rule does not prevent you from qualifying under the physical presence test.

If you cannot prove that you are a resident, check to determine if you qualify under the physical presence test, that is, your stay in the foreign country or countries included 330 full days during a period of 12 consecutive months.

To qualify under this test, you must show you were on foreign soil 330 days (nearly 11 months) during a 12-month period. Whether you were a resident or a transient is of no importance. You have to show that you were physically present in a foreign country or countries for 330 full days during any 12-month period. The 12-month period begins with the day you set foot on foreign soil.

67

WHEN TO ELECT OUT OF INSTALLMENT REPORTING

Forgo automatic installment reporting if your current tax picture will be improved by reporting your entire profit in the year of sale.

If you sell property and will receive one or more payments in a later year or years, you must report the sale as an installment sale unless you elect otherwise.

For example, in 1985 you sell real estate for $50,000, receiving $10,000 in each of 1985, 1986, and 1987, and $20,000 in 1988. You realize a profit of $25,000, giving you a profit percentage of 50%. When the buyer pays the notes, you report the following:

	You report	
In	Payment of:	Income of:
1985	$10,000	$ 5,000
1986	10,000	5,000
1987	10,000	5,000
1988	20,000	10,000
Total	$50,000	$25,000

Automatic installment reporting generally results in less tax on your profit; since taxable payments are spread out, you are less likely to be pushed into higher tax brackets. Further, you do not have to come up with the tax money until you receive payments on the sale.

However, installment reporting may not be the best tax move. The law allows you to elect out of installment reporting. If you have capital losses to offset your gain in the year of sale, installment sale reporting may not be advantageous. In such a case you may want to elect not to report on the installment basis.

If you want to report the entire gain in the year of sale, you do so within the time for filing your return (plus extensions) for the year of sale. Thus you have until April to decide which reporting method is best for you. On Schedule D, or Form 4797, you note that you are electing not to report on the installment method if this is your choice.

An election after the due date may be made only with the consent of the IRS.

An election not to report on the installment method may be revoked only with the consent of the IRS. A revocation will not be permitted for tax avoidance purposes. The IRS has ruled that if you elect not to use the installment method because you expect the income to be offset by losses but the losses are disallowed on audit, you may not revoke the election and use the installment method. According to the IRS, the revocation has a tax avoidance purpose because installment reporting would reduce your tax.

68

CHOOSE THE RIGHT YEAR TO DEDUCT WORTHLESS SECURITIES

You may deduct as a capital loss the cost basis of securities that have become worthless. However, a loss of worthless securities is deductible only in the year the securities become completely worthless.

To prove worthlessness you must be ready to show that the stock did not become worthless in a year prior to the year you claim the deduction. You must present facts fixing the time of loss during this year. For example, the company went bankrupt, stopped doing business, and is insolvent. Despite evidence of worthlessness, such as insolvency, the stock may be considered to have some value if the company continues to do business or there are plans to reorganize the company.

If you are uncertain that the company is in a hopeless financial condition, claim the deduction anyway. This advice was given by a court: "The taxpayer is at times in a very difficult position in determining in what year to claim a loss. The only safe practice, we think, is to claim a loss for the earliest year when it may possibly be allowed and to renew the claim in subsequent years if there is a reasonable chance of its being applicable for those years."

Sometimes you can avoid the problem of proving worthlessness. If there is still a market for the security, you can sell. For example, the company is on the verge of bankruptcy, but there is some doubt about the complete worthlessness of its securities. You might sell the securities for whatever you can get for them and claim the loss on the sale. However, if the security became worthless in a prior year, a later sale will not give you a deduction in the later year.

Stock which becomes worthless is deducted as a capital loss. A sale is assumed to have occurred during the year. You may not claim a loss for stock which has lost most of its value; stock must be completely worthless in order to claim the loss.

PICK THE RIGHT YEAR TO DEDUCT BAD DEBTS

If you loan money and the debtor fails to pay, you may claim a bad debt deduction. But you must take the loss at the right time.

You must show that the debt became worthless during the year you claim the deduction. Do this by proving that the debt had some value at the end of the year before the year it became worthless. For example, to prove that the debt became worthless in 1985 you must show that it had some value at the end of 1984, that there was a reasonable hope and expectation of recovering at least part of the debt. Your personal belief, unsupported by other facts, is not enough. Would a businessman have placed some value on the debt on December 31, 1984? Further, you must show that an identifiable event, such as a bankruptcy proceeding, occurred in 1985 which caused you to conclude that the debt was worthless. You do not have to go to court to try to collect the debt if you can show that a court judgment would be uncollectable, but reasonable collection steps must be taken. You do not have to wait until the debt is due to prove worthlessness. However, your cancellation of the debt does not make it worthless. You must still show that the debt was worthless when you canceled it. Finally, you must show there is no hope the debt may have some value in a later year. You are not required to prove that there is no possibility of ever receiving payment on your debt. You are not expected to be an extreme optimist.

A debt is not deductible merely because the statute of limitations has run against the debt. Although the debtor has a legal defense against your demand for payment, he or she may still recognize an obligation to pay. A debt is deductible only in the year it becomes worthless. This event, for example, the debtor's insolvency, may have occurred even before the statute became effective.

What if your debtor recognized a moral obligation to pay in

spite of the expiration of the statute of limitations, but died before paying? His or her executor defeats your claim by raising the statute of limitations. You have a bad debt deduction in the year you make the claim against the estate.

70

DEFER TAX ON INVOLUNTARY CONVERSIONS

If your property is destroyed by a casualty or taken by a government authority, gain is realized when insurance or other compensation exceeds the adjusted basis of the property. Tax may be postponed if you elect to defer gain and invest the proceeds in replacement property.

An election gives an immediate advantage. Tax on gain is postponed and the funds that would have been spent to pay the tax may be used for other investments.

As a condition of deferring tax, the basis of the replacement property is usually fixed at the same cost basis as the converted property. As long as the value of the replacement property does not decline, tax on the gain is finally incurred when the property is sold.

To decide whether postponement of gain at the expense of a reduced basis for property is advisable, compare the tax consequences of an election with the consequences if no election is made. Assume a rental building is destroyed by fire and a proper replacement is made. Assume also that gain on the receipt of the fire proceeds is taxable at capital gain rates. An election is generally not advisable if you have capital losses to offset the gain. However, even if you have no capital losses, you may still decide not to make the election and pay capital gain tax in order to fix, for purposes of depreciation, the basis of the new property at its purchase price if future depreciation deductions will offset ordinary income taxable at a higher rate than the capital gain tax. If there is little or no difference between the two rates so that a net after-tax benefit from the depreciation would not arise, an election might be made solely to postpone the payment of tax.

You make an election by omitting the taxable gain as income on the tax return for the year gain is realized. However, attach to your return a statement giving details of the transaction, including computation of the gain and your plan to buy a replacement.

To defer tax, you must generally buy property similar or related in use to the converted property within two years after the end of the taxable year you realize any gain from the conversion. However, if realty has been condemned, the replacement period is three years after the end of the taxable year any gain was realized.

Although exact duplication is not required, the replacement must be generally similar or related in use to the converted property. If real property held for productive use in a business or for investment is converted through a condemnation or threat of condemnation, the replacement test is more liberal. A replacement merely has to be of a *like kind* to the converted property. Under the *like-kind* test, the replacement of improved property by unimproved property qualifies. Under the *related-use* test, the replacement of unimproved land for improved land does not. A replacement under the related-use test generally must be closely related in function to the destroyed property. For example, a condemned personal residence must be replaced with another personal residence. The replacement of a house rented to a tenant with a house used as a personal residence does not qualify for tax deferral; the new house is not being used for the same purpose as the condemned one. This functional test, however, is not strictly applied to conversions of rental property. Here, the role of the owner toward the properties, rather than the functional use of the buildings, is reviewed. If an owner held both properties as investments and offered similar services and took similar business risks in both, the replacement may qualify.

To defer tax, the cost of the replacement property must be equal to or exceed the net proceeds from the conversion. If replacement cost is less than the adjusted basis of the converted property, report the entire gain. If replacement cost is less than the amount realized on the conversion but more than the basis of the converted property, the difference between the amount realized and the cost of the replacement is reported as gain. You may elect to postpone tax on the balance of the reinvested gain.

71

PLAN YEAR-END CHARITABLE DONATIONS

Making an extra donation at the end of the year provides an added deduction which may lower your tax. You may deduct a gift made by check on the last day of the year even if the check is not cashed until the new year begins.

Charitable donations may be timed to give you the largest possible tax savings. If, toward the end of the year, you find that you need an extra deduction, you may make a deductible donation in late December. Doing so would be especially beneficial if you know that your tax bracket will be lower the following year. For example, if your 1984 tax bracket is 42% and you estimate that in 1985 your income will be less, your deductions will be higher, or you will be subject to a lower tax rate because of rate reductions, a donation made at the end of 1984 will provide you with a larger tax savings than an identical donation in 1985. A year-end donation of $1,000 would reduce taxes by $420 in the 42% bracket. If your tax bracket fell to 33% in 1985, a $1,000 deduction would reduce 1985 taxes by $330. On the other hand, if you anticipate that your tax bracket will be higher in the following year, you will save tax dollars by postponing a donation until the start of the new year. Using the above example, if your tax bracket should rise to 45% in 1985, a $1,000 donation would reduce 1985 taxes by $450.

If you decide to make a year-end donation, you may deduct gifts made by check as long as the check is mailed on or before December 31 and you do not post-date the check or otherwise restrict the charity from cashing it before the end of the year. You may deduct your contribution even though the charity does not receive or cash the check until the following year. If you satisfy a pledge made during the year, you may deduct it; pledges not actually paid before the end of the year are not deductible. You may also make a year-end donation by credit card and deduct the gift in that year even though you do not pay the credit card bill until the following year.

You may claim a deduction for a year-end contribution of

securities by mailing or delivering a properly endorsed certificate to the charity or its agent by December 31. You may also complete the transfer by delivering the stock certificate to your bank or broker, or to the issuing company or its agent, but if you choose any of these methods, make your delivery early in December. It may take three weeks to transfer the stock on the issuing corporation's books and the transfer to the charity's name must be made on the corporation's books by December 31.

DONATE APPRECIATED PROPERTY TO CHARITY FOR TWO TAX BENEFITS

You not only claim a deduction for the property's fair market value, you also avoid the tax that would be owed if you had sold the property to provide cash for a donation.

If you own securities, real estate, or artworks that have increased in value, you may use them to fund a substantial gift to charity while reducing your taxes. Two tax benefits, a deduction for fair market value, plus avoidance of tax on the appreciation in value, are available if certain tests are met. First, your gift must be to a public charity, such as a church, synagogue, college, or hospital. Second, to deduct fair market value, you must have owned the property more than one year before the donation. For works of art, an additional test must be met. You may claim a deduction for the artwork's fair market value if you were not the artist who created it, and if it will be used by the charity in the course of carrying out its tax-exempt functions. Thus if you give a painting to a museum that will display it in its gallaries or to a college that will use the painting in its art courses or in educational art exhibitions, you may deduct its fair market value. To support your deduction, ask the school or museum for a written statement that it plans to display the painting, sculpture, or other work of art for its students or patrons.

You may figure the reduced cost of a donation of appreciated property held long term by following these two steps:

1. Figure the tax savings which result from the deduction of the fair market value of the property. For example, you donate appreciated stock which is selling at $1000. Your top tax bracket is 45%. The value of the deduction claimed for the donations is $450.
2. Estimate the tax you would have paid on a sale of the property. Assume a tax of $106 would be due on a sale of stock at $1,000. The total tax value

of your donation is $556 ($450 + $106). The cost of your $1,000 contribution is $444 ($1,000 − $556).

The fair market value of donated securities which are traded on an exchange is the mean between the high and low sale prices on the date of the donation. If you donate art, you must get an appraisal of its value from a qualified appraiser.

The deduction for a donation of mutual fund shares is the public offering price per share on the day donated, adjusted for any price reduction available to the public in purchasing that number of shares. If you donate stock of a closely held corporation, setting market value requires an evaluation by a recognized appraiser based on financial and other data relevant to the company's worth.

Penalties may be imposed if the property is overvalued by 150% or more.

To support a deduction of more than $5,000 for property contributed after 1984, you must obtain a written appraisal of the property and attach a summary of it to your return. Appraisals are not required for publicly traded securities but you need an appraisal for nonpublicly traded securities valued at more than $10,000.

ARRANGE FOR A CURRENT CONTRIBUTION DEDUCTION AND DEFER GAIN ON YEAR-END BARGAIN SALE

Year-end bargain sales of securities to a charity may result in tax deferral.

A bargain sale for cost enables you to recover your investment while donating the appreciation in the value of the property to charity; sale for more than cost but less than fair market value enables you to recover a portion of the appreciation in value while donating the remaining value. A bargain sale is treated as part-sale, part-gift, and gain allocable to the sale element is taxable.

A bargain sale to charity made toward the end of the year may also offer a tax-saving possibility if the stock or property is delivered to the charity before the end of the year but the charity does not pay until the following year. You claim a contribution deduction in the year of delivery, but gain is not taxed until the following year. You do not report gain until you receive proceeds of the sale.

Deferral of tax on the gain might be advantageous if you anticipate that your tax bracket will be lower in the following year or you will have losses to offset the gain. Further, a deferral of tax is in effect an interest-free loan from the government. For example, on December 31, 1985, you sell stock to a philanthropy for $16,000, which is the same as your cost; the stock has a fair market value of $40,000 on the date of sale. Payment is to be made in full 30 days from the date of sale, which will be in 1986. You have made a gift of $24,000 ($40,000 value less $16,000 amount realized), which is deductible in 1985 (assuming that the stock is delivered to the charity before the end of the year). Since gain is realized on the sale part, an allocation of basis is made to figure gain. Here, 40% of basis, or $6,400, is allocated to the sale:

$$\frac{\$16,000 \ (\text{sales proceeds})}{\$40,000 \ (\text{fair market value})} = 40\%$$

Thus you have gain of $9,600 on the bargain sale: $16,000 (sales proceeds) less $6,400 (basis allocated to the sale), which is taxable in 1986 when the charity makes payment.

Arrangements to defer payment until the following year must be made before completion of the sale. Payment must not be made available to you in the year of donation as, for example, in an escrow account with no conditions preventing your receipt of the money within the year. Tax in 1985 cannot be avoided by having the charity deliver a check in 1985 with the understanding that it is not to be deposited until 1986. Further, if arrangements to delay payment until 1986 are made after the sale is transacted, you will be considered in constructive receipt of the proceeds in 1985 and taxable in that year.

USE CHARITABLE TRUSTS FOR TAX BENEFITS

Charitable trusts can benefit both favored philanthropies and you and your relatives. There are two types of charitable trusts: the charitable remainder trust and the charitable income or lead trust.

Donors tend to favor charitable remainder trusts. With a remainder trust, you can provide a future interest to a charity while keeping income for your life. You receive an immediate income tax deduction for the present value of the charity's remainder interest of the trust. On the other hand the charitable lead trust is set up to pay current income to a charity. While you may not claim a deduction for the income benefit given the charity, the lead or income trust can provide these benefits: (1) Trust income is taxed to the trust, not to you, and as the trust may claim an unlimited charitable deduction for annual payments to the charity, you, in effect, are making deductible contributions which might be barred to you as an individual if the annual ceiling limitation applied to your contribution. (2) The taxable gift of the trust remainder to your family is reduced by the value of the charity's income interest. This means that you can give your family the trust property at a substantially lower gift tax cost than if given directly. In fact, it may be possible to pass on all the property with no gift tax whatsoever if an annuity income trust is used. A charitable lead trust may even allow the owner of a closely held family business to transfer stock in the company to family members at a minimal gift tax cost. The value of the charitable lead income interest reduces the gift tax value of the remainder passing to individual beneficiaries. The deductible value of the charitable interest depends on the payments made to the charity and the length of the income term.

The payout rate of an annuity trust necessary to provide a 100% gift tax deduction must exceed 10%, which is the rate built into Treasury tables as the actuarially assumed rate of return. The exact payout rate necessary to provide a 100% deduction depends on the trust term.

No gift tax is due on the remainder passing to the relatives, although at the end of the trust term they will receive the property plus any appreciation in value as long as the trust earns enough to pay the required annuity. Similar estate tax saving is made possible by using a testamentary lead trust. A donor may establish a charitable annuity trust in a will instead of during his or her lifetime. The value of the charity's income interest is determined under the same Treasury tables applicable to inter vivos (lifetime) trusts and may be claimed as an estate tax charitable deduction. By setting a high payout rate for a fixed period of time, the estate may be able to claim an estate tax deduction equal to the trust corpus which will later be received by the donor's family free of estate tax.

75

HOW TO CHOOSE BETWEEN CHARITABLE REMAINDER TRUST AND POOLED INCOME FUND

You may want to contribute to charity while keeping income for life and perhaps for the life of some other beneficiary. You may set up a charitable remainder trust or contribute to a pooled income fund established by a favored philanthropy.

Both types of contributions offer annual income and tax savings to a donor and give the charity a remainder interest in the transferred property. However, there are important differences between remainder trusts and pooled income funds. A trust must be established either during your lifetime or in your will. Creating a trust requires careful planning and drafting by an experienced tax practitioner as the requirements for remainder trusts are highly technical. If you want to avoid paperwork, you might prefer the pooled income fund which is set up by a charity and offered to the public in the same manner as a mutual fund. Contributors are assigned units in the fund based on their share of the total value of property held in the fund. Pooled income funds are more attractive to donors able to make relatively small contributions. Because your gift to a pooled income fund is combined with the contributions of other donors, the minimum required gift may be only a few thousand dollars, as opposed to the much larger cash or property values required to make charitable remainder trusts practical. It is also easy to make further contributions to a pooled income fund by acquiring additional shares in the fund. The yearly return to the donor or other income beneficiary in a pooled income fund is based on the fund's investment performance. All the fund's income must be distributed each year, with each beneficiary's share based on the number of units held.

For high-bracket taxpayers, a remainder trust has an advantage over a pooled income fund. All payouts from a pooled income fund are taxed to the recipient as ordinary income, whereas a portion of the payout from a remainder trust may be

155

taxed as capital gain or tax-exempt income, depending on the nature of the trust income. Another advantage of remainder trusts is that the income interest may be limited to a term of up to 20 years. The specified term may be shortened if you specify certain contingencies, such as remarriage of the beneficiary. This allows a high-bracket donor to temporarily shift income to another beneficiary, such as a child attending college, and receive a charitable deduction for the value of the remainder interest that the charity will receive at the end of the specified income term. With a pooled income fund, income interests must be for the lives of one or more beneficiaries with the remainder then passing to the charity administering the fund.

Whether you choose a trust or pooled income fund, you can avoid capital gain tax on the transfer of appreciated property and may claim an income tax deduction for the present value of the charity's remainder interest as determined by Treasury tables. In both cases the deduction is based on the income beneficiaries' age and sex, and the rate of return. For pooled income funds, the rate of return used in Treasury tables is based on the fund's rate of return in prior years. The higher the return, the lower the charitable deduction.

76

DONATE A RESIDENCE TO A PHILANTHROPY

A donation of a residence may yield tax benefits, and you can also arrange to live in the house for life.

Given the phenomenal rise of real estate prices in recent years, your personal residence is likely to be among your most valuable assets. In many instances, if you were to sell the house you would realize a substantial profit. If you are 55 or over, you may avoid tax on the sale if your profit is $125,000 or less. If your situation fits these facts, the donation of your residence will have no tax appeal. However, if your prospective profit is a great deal more than $125,000 or you have already used up your $125,000 exclusion on a prior home sale, you might consider the benefits of donating the residence to a charity. You may also consider the donation of a second home or vacation home since the tax-free exclusion applies only to a principal residence. A donation of such property may give you a tax deduction and allow you to avoid tax on appreciation.

If you decide to donate a residence, several alternatives should be weighed. You might give the residence outright to a charity and claim a deduction for its fair market value. If you want to continue living in the home, you may arrange for the charity to take title at some future date. For example, you may deed a remainder interest in your home to a philanthropy to take effect after your death or after the death of your surviving spouse. You may claim an immediate deduction for the present value of the charity's future interest in the home.

In donating a residence, you may realize a sizable tax deduction without a cash outlay or immediate disposition of the property. The amount of the deduction depends on the value of the house and your age and sex. An older donor receives a larger deduction than a younger donor for a house of identical market value because the value of the charity's interest is based on the donor's life expectancy. As life expectancy decreases, the value of the charitable remainder increases.

You can also provide in your will for a charity's future interest in a residence. For example, you leave a residence to your surviving spouse for life, and at the spouse's death the house is to pass to a charity. There is no income tax deduction, but the donor's estate claims an estate tax deduction for the value of the charity's future interest.

In planning a gift of a future interest in a residence, you should be careful to give the charity an outright interest, rather than an interest in trust. An income tax deduction will be denied in this situation: You transfer a residence to a trust and direct the trustee to maintain the house for use by you and your spouse during your lifetime; upon the death of the survivor, the residence is given to the charity. The charity's interest is not deductible because the interest is not in the residence itself but in a trust. To be deductible, the charity's remainder interest must be conveyed outright and not in trust.

77

TAKE A CONTRIBUTION DEDUCTION FOR DONATING PROPERTY FOR CONSERVATION PURPOSES

The tax provides a benefit to owners of real property with historic, scenic, recreational, or environmental value who want to preserve their property for conservation purposes. By entering into a conservation easement or other binding restriction on property usage, a tax deduction may be obtained while accomplishing conservationist objectives.

You can contribute a partial interest or your entire interest in real property for conservation purposes while retaining rights to subsurface minerals.

To qualify for a deduction, you must grant a scenic easement to a government unit, public charity, or an organization they control, and the restriction must further one of these objectives: (1) preserve land areas for outdoor recreation or education of the public; (2) protect fish, wildlife, or plant habitats or similar ecosystems; (3) preserve a historically important land area or certified historic structure; (4) provide open-space easements that yield significant public benefits (giving the public visual access to a scenic panorama qualifies as a deductible open-space easement). The following types of contributions also generally qualify:

- Preserving unique natural land formations for public enjoyment.
- Maintaining a scenic ocean view from a public highway by restricting development of oceanfront property.
- Preserving woodland along federal highways for scenic purposes.
- Preserving farmland pursuant to state programs for flood control.

Contributions for conservation purposes must be in perpetuity. There must be legally enforceable restrictions which prevent you from using your property in a way that would be destructive of the intended conservation purpose. You may retain an interest in subsurface oil, gas, or minerals, but may only use mining methods with limited property impact; surface mining is specifically prohibited by statute, with this exception: Surface mining does not have to be prohibited if the surface and mining interests have been separated since June 12, 1976 and there is only a negligible possibility that surface mining will occur.

Fair market value is more difficult to determine for easements and similar property restrictions than for other types of property because they are not commonly sold in the marketplace, but are granted by gift. As a result, the value of a conservation easement or other restriction is typically determined by using a before and after comparison. Appraisals prepared by real estate experts are needed to establish these values. The value before contribution should take into account not only current use but an objective assessment of how the property could have been developed absent the restriction.

DEDUCT EXPENSES OF VOLUNTEER WORK FOR CHARITY

If you do volunteer work for a charity, you may deduct unreimbursed expenses.

If you do volunteer work for charity, keep a record of your expenses. You may deduct your unreimbursed expenses, such as commuting costs to and from the charity and other unreimbursed costs for travel authorized by the charity, including meals and lodging on overnight trips.

If you use your car, your records should show costs for gas, parking, and tolls. By keeping complete records, you have the option of deducting either your actual costs or a flat mileage rate of 12¢ a mile if that would give you a larger deduction. Parking fees and tolls are also deductible if you use the 12¢-a-mile rate. (Before 1985, the rate was 9¢ a mile.) The IRS does not allow you to deduct depreciation on a car used partly for volunteer work. Nor may you deduct a proportionate share of your general car repair and maintenance costs.

In addition to car, bus, train, and airplane costs, keep records of the following costs incurred as a volunteer: phone calls; cost of materials and supplies, such as stamps and stationery; cost of uniforms required by the charity; and expenses of attending conventions as an official delegate of the organization. These are all deductible. Unfortunately, the IRS does not allow you to deduct babysitting costs, even when they make your volunteer work possible.

PROVIDE FUNDS TO CHARITY FROM A CLOSELY HELD CORPORATION

Owners of closely held corporations can use company profits to benefit their favorite philanthropies.

If you control a corporation, you may benefit your favorite charity by having the corporation itself make a contribution to the charity. If your company has substantial earnings, you can also pass some of these funds by donating your stock which the corporation then redeems. You receive a charitable deduction for the donation of stock; the charity receives cash upon redemption. To obtain these benefits, the stock must be transferred before the redemption has been voted on. If the donation is made after the decision to redeem has been made, the redemption payments will be taxed to you on the grounds that you have merely assigned the charity the redemption proceeds to which you were entitled at the time of the gift. If the redemption has not been set in motion at the time of the gift, several courts have held that the later redemption of the charity's stock by the corporation may not be treated as dividends to the stockholders.

You might also consider providing funds to charity by donating stock of a corporation scheduled for liquidation, but this carries risks. In the case of a redemption, the IRS may tax you on the liquidation proceeds on the grounds that you are merely giving away your right to receive liquidation proceeds to which you are already entitled. Several courts have supported the IRS position in cases where, as a practical matter, the liquidation is fixed at the time of the donation. In such cases stockholders have been taxed on the liquidation proceeds despite a hypothetical possibility that the liquidation plan could be rescinded after the stock donation is made.

SET UP A TAX-DEDUCTIBLE SCHOLARSHIP FUND

You may deduct contributions to a scholarship fund even if you limit eligibility to a select group.

One way to benefit your college alma mater is by setting up a scholarship fund. The tax law allows you to claim a charitable deduction for your gift even though you limit the eligible beneficiaries to a specific group. Contributions to the fund are generally deductible even if the pool of eligible scholarship beneficiaries is limited by religion and sex. You may provide scholarships to students of a particular religion, provided that the religion is open to all on a racially nondiscriminatory basis. You may also receive a deduction for scholarship funds limited to male or female recipients.

Scholarships may also be limited to certain areas of study. One donor set up a scholarship trust for needy students of military science at a specific university. The IRS held that this limitation did not deprive the scholarship fund of its educational character.

Certain scholarship restrictions will bar a charitable deduction. For example, you may not set up a scholarship fund exclusively for relatives. Your payments would not be deductible since the grants serve private rather than public educational purposes. However, you may give your relatives preference as beneficiaries without forfeiting a deduction if the scholarship fund serves overall public educational purposes and the relatives are subject to the same standards of eligibility (for example, financial need) as other potential recipients.

BUY A CLOSELY HELD COMPANY WITH ITS OWN FUNDS OR EARNINGS

The purchase of the business may be transacted by letting the buyer pay for the business in part with the company's own funds or future earnings.

If you are negotiating the purchase of a closely held corporation holding substantial cash, you may be able to arrange the terms so that you pay only part of the purchase price, with the corporation itself paying the rest. The controlling stockholder should have his corporation redeem part of his stock; you then buy the balance of his stock. Assuming you and the seller are not related, the seller can realize capital gain on the redemption instead of a fully taxable dividend because all of his interest in the corporation is being redeemed. As you have the only outstanding stock, you are in full control of the purchased corporation.

In setting up this kind of deal, be careful that you, as the buyer, do not first assume the obligation to buy all of the seller's stock and later have the corporation redeem some of his stock. Where the redemption relieves you of the obligation to buy stock, it is treated as constructive dividend to you, and you will be taxed at ordinary income rates. To avoid this result you must show that you had no obligation to purchase the redeemed stock. For example, the sole owner of a corporation agreed to sell one of his 20 shares to a buyer for $72,000. To complete the deal, the buyer arranged outside financing enabling the corporation to redeem the remaining 19 shares. The IRS argued that the redemption was a constructive dividend to the buyer; the redemption relieved him of an obligation to buy the remaining stock. The Tax Court disagreed. The buyer was obligated to buy only one share of stock. He had no obligation to buy the rest. The redemption was not a constructive dividend. The IRS later agreed to the decision.

HOW TO BUY PROPERTY OWNED BY A CORPORATION

If you are interested in buying property owned by a corporation, there are alternative ways of making the purchase. Each alternative has different tax consequences.

You may buy the property from the corporation or you may acquire ownership of the corporation itself by purchasing its stock. As a practical matter you may not have a choice, as the seller may insist on either a direct purchase of the property or a stock purchase. After a stock purchase, you may continue operation of the corporation or liquidate the corporation and thereby obtain direct ownership of the property.

If you are free to negotiate either a stock or asset acquisition, consider these guideline:

1. How does the price of the property compare with its tax basis on the books of the corporation? If the purchase price is more than its tax basis, try to buy the property directly. Your tax basis for the property is the price you pay and will affect depreciation deductions as well as the amount of gain or loss on your future disposition of the property.

If you buy the stock, you may be held to low book values unless you meet the special rules under which you may buy the corporation's stock, liquidate the corporation, and then step up the basis of the assets to market value.

If the purchase price is lower than the tax basis, try to buy the stock. The corporation's basis for the property will give you bigger depreciation deductions. And if you sell the property later at a profit, you can cut the gain or even get a book loss with the use of the higher basis.

Does the corporation hold depreciable property which is subject to recapture rules? If you buy the stock and the corporation later sells the asset, it may incur ordinary income on the sale. In this case you may want to avoid a stock purchase and insist on a purchase of the property directly. On your purchase, the seller, not you, will incur tax on the ordinary income from recapture.

2. What are the tax benefits if you continue the same corporate form? Consider the tax advantages of starting your business with the seller's accounting methods, methods of computing depreciation, depletion, or amortization, carryback or carryforward of capital losses and net operating losses.

Be aware of these problems if you decide to buy the stock: Has the corporation hidden or contingent liabilities, especially unpaid tax bills, for which you may be liable? Protect yourself against any loss you may suffer from these liabilities by obtaining a warranty from the seller. See if there are unfavorable contracts or restrictions, such as burdensome contracts with unions, officers, or pension plans.

There may be a hidden tax cost to you if you contemplate selling any of the corporation's property (other than its inventory). This will occur if the corporation's basis for its assets is significantly lower than market value. By paying market value for the stock, you are in effect buying an income tax liability should the corporation later sell the assets. The corporation is taxed on its gain (market value less basis), and you in turn are taxed on the proceeds if they are distributed to you as dividends.

This cost may be avoided by liquidating the corporation within certain time limits which would give you a market value basis for the former corporation's assets. It may also be avoided, of course, by purchasing the assets directly, rather than the corporate stock. Or you may demand from the seller an adjustment to the stock purchase price to reflect the future tax liability.

83

CONSIDER A COVENANT NOT TO COMPETE WHEN YOU BUY A BUSINESS

For a buyer of a business, a covenant not to compete offers not only legal protection but also tax advantages by giving a deduction for part of the purchase.

When you buy a business, your investment is not deductible except for amounts allocated to depreciable property. However, if you can arrange for part of the purchase price to be allocated to a covenant not to compete, you may deduct the amount paid for the covenant over its duration. If there is no specific covenant, the IRS will assume the entire purchase price is for the seller's tangible assets plus goodwill, and the price allocated to goodwill is not deductible. For tax purposes, it is not enough to include a covenant in the contract. Make sure that a specific portion of the purchase price is allocated to the covenant.

For example, you buy the business of your competitor. To protect yourself from competition and to deduct part of the purchase price, you should have your attorney draft the following type of covenant for inclusion in the sales contract: "Seller agrees that, for a period of five years after this sale, he will not, without Buyer's prior written consent, directly or indirectly own, manage, operate, control, participate in, or serve as an officer, employee, or partner in any business which directly or indirectly competes with the company or its products. Seller agrees that this covenant not to compete is materially significant to this sales agreement, and therefore agrees that $_____ of the $_____ purchase price is allocable to this covenant not to compete."

You will probably meet seller opposition to your request for a covenant because he or she must report the payments allocated to the covenant as ordinary income. However, if you persist in demanding the covenant and there is a real business justification for it, your contract will be a secure basis for your deduction.

Sometimes a seller may claim capital gain treatment for the

entire sales proceeds even though the sales contract includes a covenant not to compete. If the IRS examines the seller's tax return, he or she may claim that the covenant was without economic substance, that there was no real threat of competition, and that you insisted on the covenant purely for tax purposes. Such a claim might lead to an IRS examination of your treatment of the deal.

However, there are court decisions preventing the seller from challenging the covenant's value. Some courts will not disregard a covenant clause unless there is proof of undue influence, fraud, or duress. The Tax Court will look at the circumstances surrounding the contract to see if a covenant was bargained for and had business purpose. To upset the contract a seller or the IRS would have to have evidence that the covenant lacked economic reality.

WRITE A PARTNERSHIP AGREEMENT TO AVOID TAX PROBLEMS

Your partnership agreement is a vital instrument that should direct how the business is to operate and how certain tax problems are to be treated. In the absence of such provisions, the law may supply rules differing widely from your intentions.

Although there are generally no immediate tax consequences on the organization of a partnership, the partnership agreement should anticipate and resolve tax problems that may arise in your future operations, such as profit and loss ratios for different partnership income and deduction items, the treatment of salary and interest payments, the treatment of contributed property for depreciation and sales purposes, and the treatment of partnership interests upon withdrawal from the partnership.

Partnership allocations of income and loss to each partner generally are based on the partner's individual interest in the partnership. However, partners may agree to make special allocations disproportionate to their capital contributions. To make a special allocation, they may amend a partnership agreement at any time until the due date of the partnership tax return for that year. An allocation, as well as any item of income, gain, loss, deduction, or credit, will be recognized if the partner receiving the allocation can show that it has substantial economic effect. If an allocation made by the partnership is set aside, a partner's share of the income, gain, loss, deduction, or credit is determined according to his or her interest in the partnership.

Contributed property. A partner, instead of investing cash, may contribute property to the partnership. If, however, there is a difference between his or her cost or tax basis for the property and its present market value, the law requires the partnership to allocate the differences in order to level out the differences. For example, in forming the AJ Partnership, Adams invested $30,000 in cash and Jones invested a building that cost $15,000 but is now worth $30,000. The basis of the building to the partnership is $15,000, even though, for nontax purposes,

Jones is credited in his capital account with a $30,000 investment. This disparity between the partnership basis and crediting Jones with a $30,000 capital account creates the following drawbacks: if the property is sold shortly thereafter for $30,000, the partnership has a $15,000 gain and without an allocation Adams might be taxed on half or $7,500. This is patently unfair to her; she is being taxed for a gain that really belongs to Jones. Even if the property is not sold, depreciation is figured on the lower tax basis of $15,000, depriving Adams of the larger depreciation deduction she would normally expect. To overcome these inequities, the law requires the partnership to level out these differences. For example, if the property was sold, all gain allocated to a price of $30,000 or less is Jones's. That part of the gain allocated to a price over $30,000 is divided between the two partners. Similarly depreciation is allocated to Adams to the extent that the deduction would have been based on fair market value. Here, all or substantially all of the depreciation would be allocated to Adams. The Treasury is to release regulations explaining these adjustments.

Contributing property subject to a mortgage. If you are planning to transfer mortgaged property to the partnership, check to see that you do not incur a hidden tax liability which could occur if the mortgage exceeds the basis of the property that you contribute. On the contribution of mortgaged property, each partner is considered to have assumed the mortgage pro rata. The proportionate decrease in your liability is considered a distribution of cash which reduces your basis. If your partnership basis is less than this reduction, you have realized taxable gain.

Agreement on salaries and interest payments. Partners' salaries and interest payments on borrowing can be treated in one of two ways: as distributions of profits or as guaranteed payments. Your partnership agreement can determine which method is to be used. Guaranteed payments are treated as if made to complete outsiders; they are deducted whether or not the partnership has sufficient income to cover them. They are not considered salary payments for the purposes of withholding taxes or self-employment taxes. However, for self-employment purposes, they are included along with a partner's distributive share of the partnership income as well as self-employment income. Note that although a guaranteed payment is a deduction to the partnership, it is not income to the partner at the time received but at the end of the partnership year in which the payment is made. Hence the partnership salary is taxable to the partner at the same time that his or her share of the partnership profits is taxable.

For property contributed to a partnership after March 31, 1984 in taxable years ending after such date, the taxable character of a sale of certain property contributed by a partner is the same as if the partner had sold the property before it was contributed. If property contributed is an unrealized receivable, any gain or loss recognized by the partnership on the disposition of the receivable will be treated as ordinary income or loss. Contributed inventory items are subject to similar rule only if the disposition occurs within five years of the date the property was contributed to the partnership.

If a contributing partner had an unrecognized capital loss on contributed property, any loss recognized by the partnership on the disposition of the property within five years will be treated as a loss from the sale of a capital asset to the extent of the contributing partner's unrecognized loss.

SHOULD YOU OPERATE YOUR BUSINESS AS AN S CORPORATION?

The legal advantages of a corporation are available without the payment of corporate tax. By filing an S election to report corporate earnings and losses, you may keep the election as long as it benefits you or for as short a period as one year.

As a stockholder, you agree to report on your personal tax return your share of the corporation's undistributed taxable income as ordinary income. Actual cash distributions are treated as dividends but are not reduced by the dividend exclusion. The dividend exclusion applies to dividend distributions out of earnings and profits held by the company before the election.

Items of income, deductions, losses, and credits of the corporation pass through to the shareholders in the same general manner as the character of such items of a partnership passes through to partners. Thus, for example, such items as tax-exempt interest and capital gains and losses pass through and retain their character in the hands of shareholders.

An S election may be advisable for a new corporation which anticipates losses at the start. The shareholders may deduct their share of these losses on their personal tax returns.

New law changes facilitate the use of S corporations by easing restrictions on the number of shareholders permissible in the corporation and on the receipt of investment income. Corporations that do not have accumulated earnings and profits from years prior to the S election are not subject to a passive income test. This means that investment holdings for such S corporations will not jeopardize the S election. An S company may have up to 35 shareholders.

The new law has eliminated a tax saving opportunity for new corporations. In the past a new corporation could adopt a fiscal year in order to defer income. Starting in 1983, new corporations must report on a calendar year unless a business purpose can be shown for a fiscal year or the fiscal year results in no more than a three-month deferral of income for shareholders owning more than 50% of the stock.

Finally there is this limitation to consider: For S elections made after September 28, 1982, owners of more than 2% of the stock will realize taxable income for receiving fringe benefit coverage such as in employee group insurance and accident and health plans. This tax rule does not apply until 1988 to shareholders of an S corporation existing as of September 28, 1982, provided the corporation does not have passive income of more than 20% of gross receipts or does not have a change of majority stockholders after 1982.

86

HOW TO CHOOSE AN ACCOUNTING BASIS

The tax method you choose to report business income gives you opportunities to delay or accelerate income.

You may report your business income on either the accrual or cash basis even if you report your nonbusiness income on the cash basis. If you have more than one business, you may use a different accounting method for each business. If you have inventories, you must use the accrual basis.

The cash basis has this advantage over other accounting methods: you may defer reporting income by postponing receipt of income. For example, if 1985 is a high-income year, you might extend the date of payment of some of your customers' bills until 1986. But make certain that you avoid the constructive receipt rule explained below. You may also postpone the payment of current expenses to a year in which the deduction gives you a greater tax saving.

Under the cash basis, you report income items in the taxable year they are received; you deduct all expenses in the taxable year they are paid. Income is also included under the cash basis if it is "constructively" received, that is, an amount is credited to your account, subject to your control, or set apart for you and may be drawn by you at any time. For example, in 1984 you receive a paycheck but you do not cash it until 1985. The check is taxable income in 1984.

In general, you deduct expenses in the year you pay them. If expenses are paid by credit card, you deduct them in the year you charge them. If expenses are paid through a "pay by phone" account with a bank, you deduct them in the year the bank sends the check. This date is reported by the bank on its monthly statement.

Under the accrual basis, you report income that has been earned, whether or not received, unless a substantial contingency affects your right to collect the income. You deduct costs and expenses that have been incurred, whether or not paid, if economic performance has occurred. Under the economic performance test, you may generally not deduct accrued expenses for a third party's services until those services are performed. The Treasury is to provide rules under which regularly recurring business expenses may be deducted before the year of economic performance. But accrued interest, salaries, and other expenses payable to members of your family and other controlled relationships are deductible only in the year of payment.

The accrual basis has this advantage over the cash basis: it generally gives a more even and balanced financial report of your business activity.

TAKE ADVANTAGE OF BUSINESS LOSSES

You can turn a business loss into cash by applying this year's loss to other tax years.

A loss incurred in your profession or unincorporated business is deducted from other income reported on Form 1040. If the loss (plus any casualty loss) exceeds your current income, the excess loss may be first carried back three years and *then* forward 15 years until it is used up. A loss carried back to the prior year reduces income of that year and entitles you to a refund. A loss applied to a later year reduces income for that year.

If you have incurred a loss at the end of a tax year, the tax law provides a method of obtaining a fast refund if you decide to carry back the loss. You file Form 1045, called a "quick refund" claim. Do not attach it to your tax return; file the claim separately. But do not file it later than 12 months after the end of your tax year. The IRS will usually allow or reject your claim within 90 days from the time you file Form 1045.

You may elect to forgo the carryback and instead just carry forward losses. The carryforward period is 15 years under the election. The election is irrevocable.

You will generally make the election if you expect greater tax savings by carrying the loss forward rather than first carrying it back. You might also make the election if you are concerned you might be audited for earlier years if you carry back a loss for a refund. You make the election by attaching a statement to this effect to your return, which must be filed by the due date plus extensions.

WHEN TO FORGO THE ELECTION TO EXPENSE BUSINESS EQUIPMENT

Electing to expense will save more taxes in the first year, but it may mean fewer write-offs over the life of the equipment.

You may elect to deduct up to $5,000 of the cost of business equipment. Under this election, all or part of the cost for personal property used in business may be written off in the year of acquisition instead of depreciating the cost under ACRS (accelerated cost recovery system). The election is limited to personal property used in business and eligible for the investment credit.

To the extent the cost of property is expensed, no investment credit is allowed. The portion of the cost not expensed is recovered under ACRS.

Whether it is advisable to forgo the credit for expensing depends on a taxpayer's position in the year the property is placed in service. Expensing is generally not advisable because of the loss of the investment credit on the amount expensed. However, there may be circumstances under which it is advantageous to forgo the credit. For example, in an unusually high-income year, the cash flow generated by tax savings from expensing may be more important than the lost credit, especially if the first-year savings is invested at a rate of return which may make up for the lost credit.

To claim first-year expensing for a business car or home computer after June 18, 1984, you must use it more than 50% of the time for business. Otherwise first-year expensing and ACRS is disallowed and you must use straight-line depreciation.

Here is a comparison of the tax savings with and without expensing from a machine (five-year property) costing $10,000 in 1985. The figures assume that your tax bracket is 50% in 1985. Basis of the machine is reduced by one-half of the investment credit before figuring ACRS deductions.

TAX SAVINGS WITH EXPENSING

Year	Investment credit	Tax savings from expensing plus ACRS	Total tax savings
1	$ 500	$2,856	$3,356
2		523	523
3		499	499
4		499	499
5		499	499
			$5,376

TAX SAVINGS WITHOUT EXPENSING

Year	Investment credit	Tax savings from ACRS	Total tax savings
1	$1,000	$ 713	$1,713
2		1,045	1,045
3		998	998
4		998	998
5		998	998
			$5,752

SHOULD YOU TRADE IN BUSINESS EQUIPMENT?

New business equipment is often partially financed by trading in old equipment. For tax purposes, a trade-in may not be a good decision.

If the market value of the equipment is below its adjusted basis, it is generally preferable to sell the equipment to realize an immediate deductible loss. You may not deduct a loss on a trade-in. However, if you do trade, the potential deduction reflected in the cost basis of the old equipment is not forfeited. The undepreciated basis of the old property becomes part of the basis of the new property and may be depreciated. Therefore, in deciding whether to trade in or sell when a loss may be realized, determine whether you will get a greater tax reduction by taking an immediate loss on a sale or by claiming larger depreciation deductions.

If the fair market value of the old equipment exceeds its adjusted basis, you have a potential gain. To defer tax on this gain, you may want to trade in the equipment for new equipment. Your decision to sell or trade in will generally be based on a comparison between: (1) tax imposed on an immediate sale and larger depreciation deductions taken on the cost basis of the new property; and (2) the tax consequences of a trade-in in which the tax is deferred but reduced depreciation deductions are taken on a lower cost basis of the property. In making this comparison you will have to estimate your future income and tax rates. Also pay attention to the possibility that gain on the sale may be taxed as ordinary income under the depreciation recapture rules.

The tax consequences of a trade-in may not be avoided by first selling the used property to the dealer who sells you the new property. The IRS will disregard the sale made to the same dealer from whom you purchase the new equipment. The two transactions will be treated as one trade-in.

HOW TO COMPLETELY LIQUIDATE YOUR BUSINESS

A liquidation of your corporation calls for expert planning to avoid double tax and ensure capital gain treatment.

If your corporation holds appreciated assets, you want to plan a transaction that will involve only one tax at capital gain rates. The most direct method is a sale of your stock in the corporation to a third party. However, the buyer may be unwilling to buy the stock, so that a sale of the assets is required. Special 12 month liquidation rules generally allow the sale of the assets without tax consequences to the corporation. Tax is realized by you as a stockholder at capital gain rates upon the corporation's liquidation. To come within the 12-month liquidation rules, the corporation must adopt a formal plan of complete liquidation before the sale of its assets (although sales negotiations may begin prior to adoption of the plan) and it must distribute all assets, except those needed to satisfy creditor claims within the 12-month period beginning on the date of the adoption of the plan of liquidation. Reasonable amounts may be set aside for contingent claims as well as fixed claims. The corporation may not retain assets for the satisfaction of stockholders' claims on their shares. Thus, if certain stockholders cannot be located within the 12-month period, the corporation should make their pro rata distribution to an independent trustee or a special escrow account for the benefit of those stockholders.

When you liquidate your corporation and receive its assets in exchange for your stock, you treat the receipt of corporate assets as if you had sold your stock. That is, you will generally have capital gain if the value of the property received exceeds the cost basis of your stock which has been held long term. If it is less than the cost basis of your stock, you will have a capital loss. The basis of the property received from the corporation is equal to the fair market value of the property at the time of the transfer.

A corporation that distributes depreciable property as part of the liquidation proceeds incurs tax on the ordinary-income element present in the asset under the recapture rules.

If, after receiving the property from a liquidating corporation, you put the property into a new corporation, you run the risk that the IRS may treat the liquidation and reincorporation as a tax-free reorganization and not allow the new corporation to fix as the basis of the property its fair market value at the time of the liquidation. Basis would be limited to the basis of the property on the books of the old corporation. In addition, your receipt of cash or securities on the liquidation would be taxed as "boot" at ordinary income rates.

HOW TO PLAN A SPECIAL ONE-MONTH LIQUIDATION

A one-month liquidation can be useful in effecting a tax-free liquidation of a corporation which holds appreciated property, such as a building, if you now want to operate as an individual or in partnership.

If your corporation does not have earnings and profits but holds only appreciated property, such as a building, you can liquidate without paying tax at the time of liquidation (unless there is an ordinary-income element subject to depreciation recapture rules). Tax on the appreciation is postponed until you later sell the building at a profit. If the corporation has earnings and profits, or if it distributes cash, stock, or securities, part of the liquidation is taxed. Ordinary income is realized to the extent of earnings and profits held by the corporation. The remainder of the gain is taxed as capital gain to the extent that the value of securities plus cash, exceeds earnings and profits.

There are advantages to this type of liquidation: you will be taxed on gain from the liquidation only to a limited extent, and if there is no cash or certain securities received, all of the gain will be taxed at capital gain rates.

There are these disadvantages: (1) if there is substantial cash or certain securities distributed, you will have to report gain to the extent of accumulated and current earnings as ordinary income; (2) the basis of the assets in your hands is usually lower than it would be in a regular liquidation so that there will be a lower depreciation basis or more taxable profit if you decide to sell the asset; (3) the one-month limitation is rigidly enforced, and if you fail to meet the deadline, you will lose the benefits. However, loss of the one-month liquidation benefits will, in most cases, result in all of the gain's being taxed at capital gain rates. In one case a stockholder's failure to file a necessary notice disqualified a one-month election.

The IRS does not require that the corporation be dissolved during the one-month period, but only that the "status of liquidation" exists during that period. A status of liquidation exists when the corporation ceases to be a going concern and its activities are merely for the purpose of winding down its affairs, paying its debts, and distributing any remaining balance to its stockholders. The corporation is permitted to retain necessary cash to pay contingent liabilities and expenses after the end of the one-month period.

WHEN TO PARTIALLY LIQUIDATE YOUR BUSINESS

You may be able to withdraw funds at capital gain rates when you contract part of your business operations and distribute funds in return for cancellation of part of your stock.

Partial liquidations occur when a corporation redeems part of your shares in the process of contracting or curtailing part of its business operations. To qualify for capital gain on the distribution, several tests must be met. First, you must establish a formal plan setting forth the distribution of assets in redemption of part of your stock. Second, the distribution must occur within the taxable year the plan is adopted or within the following taxable year. You must also show that the company was actively engaged in conducting at least two businesses and that the distribution is attributed to the cessation of operations of one of those business activities. Further, the curtailed business must also have been conducted by the corporation during the five-year period preceding the partial liquidation.

If the corporation distributes appreciated property as part of the partial liquidation, it may have to recognize a gain (to the extent the property's value exceeds the corporation's basis) on the distribution. This is true even if you qualify for capital gain under the above rules. However, the corporation will not incur tax on any gain provided that you owned at least 10% of the outstanding stock during the five years preceding the liquidation, or if shorter, the period of the corporation's existence. For purposes of determining 10% ownership during the applicable period, you are considered to have owned shares owned by your spouse, children, and other relatives under a constructive ownership rule.

A partial liquidation can be based on the sale of a building that is owned and managed by the corporation. However, a building that is managed by independent contractors may not meet the active business test. If a building subject to a mortgage is sold, only the net value of the building qualifies as a distribution in partial liquidation.

If you are planning to receive a distribution of company assets which you intend to sell, it is vital to have the corporation distribute the assets *before* the sale is negotiated. In one case stockholders intended a partial liquidation and sale, but through poor planning allowed the company to make the sale and distribute the sale proceeds. A double tax was incurred. The company was taxed on the sale and the shareholders were taxed on the distribution. The company argued that no corporate tax should be incurred because the sale was part of an integrated plan of partial liquidation. A court rejected the argument. Whether the sale and later distribution of the proceeds were integral parts of one plan was of no consequence. The issue was the taxability of the sale proceeds, not the taxability of the distribution. If the company had distributed the building to the shareholders under a plan of partial liqiudation, no tax on gain to the corporation would have resulted. The shareholders could have then sold the building and reported the gain. But the way the transaction was actually handled resulted in an assessment of tax against the corporation which could have been avoided. The court agreed that this result was contrary to the company's intention. If the court had the power to decide the case on equitable principles, it would order judgment for the company. But the tax consequences of partial liquidations depend on the formal manner in which the transactions were arranged, and under the law, partial liquidations remain a tax trap for the unwary.

HOW TO QUALIFY FOR CAPITAL GAINS ON REDUCING YOUR INVESTMENT IN YOUR COMPANY

As a stockholder in a corporation, it is to your advantage to convert potential dividend income to capital gain income. Planning a redemption of stock can achieve this goal.

In arranging a redemption, you have to make sure that the distribution on the cancellation of your stock is not treated as a dividend taxable at ordinary income rates. To qualify for capital gain, you must satisfy certain technical provisions. Generally, you will realize capital gain if all of your stock is redeemed. If only part of your stock is redeemed, the redemption must meet certain percentage tests to assure capital gain. Pay special attention to the tests applied when members of your family also own stock in the corporation. To ensure capital gain if you are leaving a family corporation, you must make certain to sever your interest in the business. This may be difficult if remaining shareholders are related to you; stock held by your spouse, children, grandchildren, or parents may be treated as yours. Thus a redemption of your stock may be taxed as a dividend since your family continues to hold shares in the corporation. To avoid this result, you may file an agreement with the IRS that you will notify it of any subsequent acquisition of an interest in the corporation. The "family attribution" rules are then waived, and the redemption is eligible for capital gain treatment.

Gain may later be treated as ordinary income if you acquire any interest (including an interest as officer, director, or employee), other than an interest as creditor, within ten years from the date of the redemption of your shares, except by inheritance.

In one case a redemption which tentatively qualified for capital gain treatment became subject to ordinary income tax when the retired stockholder became president of a corporation while acting as executor of his father's estate. His role as president, not as executor, violated the redemption rules. The violation would have existed even if he had discontinued serving as president after the estate was settled.

In addition to potential problems with family attribution, you are also considered to own the stock owned by: (1) partnerships and estates to the extent of your proportional interest therein; (2) trusts in which you have an interest; and (3) corporations in which you own 50% or more of the stock to the extent of your percentage of stock ownership. These constructive ownership interests cannot be waived as in the case of family attribution.

94

SECURE CAPITAL GAIN ON THE SALE OF A PATENT

Whether you are an inventor or a financial backer of an invention, you can plan for capital gain return.

A special law gives inventors and their backers an opportunity to qualify for capital gain on the sale of patents. There are advantages to qualifying under this special law: Long-term gain is not dependent on any holding period. The invention can be transferred even before an application for the patent is made. The sale can be either in the form of an outright sale, an exclusive license, or an assignment or royalty agreement.

If you are an inventor, you must transfer all substantial rights in the patent to a party who is not your employer and who is not a close relative, such as your spouse, parent, or child. Also, you cannot sell the patent to a corporation in which you have an interest or to certain trusts. Make sure you do not limit the period or duration of the patent to a period less than the remaining life of the patent or restrict the patent license use to a particular industry. If you do, you will forfeit capital gain treatment. You can keep the right to prohibit sublicensing or subassignment of rights. You can also keep a security interest, such as a lien and reserve rights in case of forfeiture for nonperformance.

If you are a financial backer and are anticipating capital return on a patent, make sure you buy all of the substantial rights to the patent before the invention is reduced to practice. You may not qualify for capital gain under the special rule if, at the time you bought your interest, you were the employer or a related part of the inventor.

If you cannot meet the special rule, for example, if you bought the patent after it was put into operation, you still may qualify for capital gain if your interest meets the general capital gain tests. That is, you hold the patent as a capital asset or as a

"Section 1231" asset, and you dispose of it in a transaction that is considered a sale or exchange after a long-term holding period. However, one court decision held that capital gain is available only if the special rule is met.

95

MINIMIZE TAXES ON LUMP-SUM PENSION PLAN DISTRIBUTIONS

Recipients of lump-sum distributions from qualified plans have the choice of paying tax now or rolling over the distribution and paying tax later. For most taxpayers, it is advisable to pay now because of exceptionally low tax rates under a special method.

If you receive a distribution of your entire pension plan account from your employer's qualified retirement plan within one year and you are at least age 59½ or disabled, or have retired, resigned, or been discharged, you are faced with a choice: pay tax now or pay it later. While it is generally true that it is better to defer taxes, it may not be advisable in this case. The reason: A lump-sum distribution of benefits qualifies for a special ten-year averaging method which means that if tax is paid now, it will be at unusually low rates.

The one-time tax under the ten-year averaging rule is figured separate and apart from the tax on your other income. The effect of the averaging method is to tax the distribution as if it were received evenly over a ten-year period. The tax itself is taken from the single's tax rate schedule, regardless of your marital or head-of-household status. Use of ten-year averaging gives a low effective rate of tax. Sample effective rates are:

Amount of distribution	Effective tax rate for 1985
Under $20,000	5.5%
$25,000	7.2%
$30,000	8.4%
$40,000	10.5%
$50,000	11.8%
$75,000	13.8%
$100,000	14.6%

Instead of paying tax now, you may defer tax by making a tax-free rollover; simply transfer your lump-sum distribution to an IRA or to a qualified plan of a new employer within 60 days of receipt. When payouts from IRAs are made, they are taxed at ordinary-income rates; you lose forever your right to ten-year averaging if you roll over your distribution to an IRA. You cannot defer indefinitely the payment of income tax on the lump sum. You must begin to receive distributions at age 70½ or be subject to a penalty tax for insufficient withdrawals. Before making a tax-free rollover, figure your current tax on the lump-sum distribution. Compare it with an estimate of tax payable on a later disposition of the rolled over account.

Rules for making rollovers are as follows: If you receive one payment from your plan which includes all you are owed, the 60-day period starts with the date of that payment. If the distribution is in several payments, the 60-day period starts from the date of the last payment, provided all the payments are made within one taxable year. For example, you retire in July 1985 and receive a partial distribution from your company plan. You are told that you will receive the balance by December 1985. Provided all payments are received before the end of 1985, the payments received in July and December are considered a lump-sum distribution eligible for rollover. You have 60 days from the date of the final December payment to complete the rollover.

Your employer's retirement plan may invest in a limited amount of life insurance. The insurance contract may then be distributed to you as part of a lump-sum retirement distribution. Tax on a lump sum may generally be avoided through a rollover to an IRA or other qualified plan. However, you may not roll over a life insurance contract to an IRA. The law specifically bars investment of IRA funds in life insurance contracts. Thus if you receive a lump-sum distribution of cash and a life insurance contract, the cash (less your own contributions) may be rolled over tax free to an IRA. The insurance contract may not be rolled over, and the value of the contract, less your contribution, is taxed in the year of distribution. However, if within 60 days of the distribution you take a position with another company which has a qualified plan that does not bar investments in life insurance contracts, you may make a tax-free rollover of the insurance contract to the new employer's plan.

A rollover does not allow you to avoid payment of tax. It merely postpones payment to some future date. The decision to make a rollover involves an evaluation of present and future needs, as well as the tax consequences of the rollover. If you need the funds immediately, perhaps to buy a retirement home or to start a business for your retirement years, you will not roll over the distribution. If you receive a lump-sum distribution because your plan terminates but you were not a plan participant for at least five years, you may not use ten-year averaging and should make a rollover to avoid immediate tax. Even if you do qualify for ten-year averaging but do not have a pressing need for the funds, you may consider a rollover, weighing the tax consequences of postponing tax through rollovers with the payment of immediate tax using ten-year averaging.

EXAMPLES—

1. In 1985 you receive a lump-sum distribution of $100,000. You made no contribution to the sum. If you decide not to roll over the amount to an IRA, the tax under ten-year averaging is $14,700, leaving you $85,300. If you rolled over the amount to an IRA, you would defer tax but lose the right to use ten-year averaging. This might prove costly if an emergency required you to withdraw the entire amount from the IRA. For example, two years after you roll over you need the funds from the IRA account which has grown to $125,000. If the amount was subject to the following tax rates, you would net as follows:

Tax rate	Net
30%	$87,500
40%	$76,000
50%	$62,500

If you had not made the rollover and had invested the $85,300 in tax-exempts paying around 12%, your fund would have been about $105,327 in two years. Here the better choice would have been not to roll over.

Assume you retire at 65 and do not currently need the $100,000. You roll it over. When you reach 70 the value of the fund is $176,000. If you withdraw the amount as a lump sum, you net as follows:

Tax rate	Net
30%	$123,200
40%	$105,600
50%	$88,000

If you had not rolled over the $100,000, you would have netted $85,300 which, if invested in tax-exempts returning 12%, would provide $150,327 at age 70.

2. Assume you retire at age 60 and receive $100,000. If you decide not to roll over, the net amount of $85,300 invested in tax-exempts at 12% will grow in ten years to $265,000. If you roll over $100,000 at 12%, it will grow to $310,600 at age 70. If, at that time, you withdraw the amount as a lump sum, you would net the following:

Tax rate	Net
30%	$217,000
40%	$186,000
50%	$155,000

Based on the above projections, it is generally unwise to roll over if you are planning to take your account in a lump sum. On the other hand a rollover may prove more advantageous if you allow the fund to accumulate tax free and then withdraw the fund over your life expectancy. However, even here, paying the tax immediately may return more if you invest in instruments yielding a substantial tax-free return.

You do not have to make a rollover of your entire account; you may roll over part of the distribution and keep part of it. The rolled over portion is tax free. The amount not rolled over is currently taxable. However, because you have rolled over a portion of the funds, you may not use special ten-year averaging or capital gain treatment. If you had not made a rollover, you would be allowed to use these methods.

96

USE TAX REDUCTIONS TO FUND PERSONAL RETIREMENT SAVINGS

Establish an individual retirement account to accumulate funds for retirement and save on current taxes.

For retirement security, you can supplement Social Security benefits and company pension plans. The tax law gives you the opportunity to set up IRAs with the following benefits:

Contributions to an IRA fund are deductible up to a maximum contribution of $2000 per year. (If earnings are less than $2000, the deduction may not exceed earnings.) If you are in the 32% bracket, a contribution of $2000 reduces your tax by $640. In other words, of your $2000, $640 would have been used to pay taxes had you not set up an IRA. Had you merely intended to invest $2000 of pre-tax income in another type of investment, you would only have had $1360 after taxes to invest.

Income earned on the account is not taxed until the funds are withdrawn. Tax savings and tax-free interest compounding can produce the following retirement funds:

$2,000 invested annually for	Rate of interest compounded daily		
	8%	12% gives you	16%
10 years	$32,100	$48,150	$64,200
20 years	$104,346	$156,519	$208,692
30 years	$266,942	$400,413	$533,884

Contribution years	Taxes saved if you were in tax bracket of		
	30%	40%	50%
10	$6,000	$8,000	$10,000
20	$12,000	$16,000	$20,000
30	$18,000	$24,000	$30,000

While IRAs offer you tax savings and investment opportunities, there are restrictions to consider: You may not start withdrawing from the account until you reach age 59½ or become disabled. If you do take money out of the account, or even borrow using the account as collateral, you are subject to a penalty tax. Further, you *must* start withdrawing from the account by age 70½, and contributions in the year in which you become age 70½ are not deductible. All distributions from IRAs are fully taxable as ordinary income. Finally, excess contributions are subject to penalties.

97

CHOOSE THE BEST TYPE OF RETIREMENT PLAN

If your business does not yet have a qualified retirement plan, you may set one up to gain tax benefits and increase employee goodwill.

You may have your company establish a retirement plan to provide current tax deductions for contributions, tax-free accumulation of earnings on the contributions, and special tax breaks for reporting retirement benefits.

A corporation may choose from several types of qualified retirement plans: pension plan, profit-sharing plan, stock-bonus plan, thrift plan, or a combination of plans. A pension plan is designed to provide a fixed benefit upon retirement. There are two types of pension plans. In a defined benefit plan, the level of benefits is fixed and contributions are geared to provide those benefits at retirement. In a defined contribution plan, the contributions are fixed, and benefits depend on the size of the contributions and the number of years before retirement. Both types of pension plans differ from profit-sharing plans in that contributions must be made, regardless of profits.

If your corporation chooses a defined benefit plan, the first step is deciding on a formula for determining benefits. Benefits are often based on years of service and a percentage of earnings over a certain period. For example, a plan may provide for a pension equal to a small percentage (1% or 2%) of an employee's average compensation during the last five years before retirement multiplied by years of service. For high earners, the pension allowed by the plan may have to be reduced because the law limits the annual benefit payable by defined benefit plans.

Once the benefit formula is determined, the company will actuarially compute the level of contributions needed to provide the funds to pay the anticipated benefits. Contributions must be made, regardless of profits. To determine annual contributions, an actuary will consider your age, earnings, and years before reaching retirement. Earnings of the fund may also affect contributions. If the fund earns more than the rate assumed when the plan was set up, the company may decrease its contributions; the IRS could require increased contributions if the plan does not earn as much as had been assumed.

In a defined contribution plan, such as a money-purchase pension plan, the company commits itself to make a fixed annual contribution, regardless of profits. For example, a money-purchase plan may require contributions equal to 10% of each participant's annual salary. Contributions plus earnings on the fund will determine benefits.

In general, the money-purchase plan is favored if the employees are relatively young, since retirement benefits depend on the number of years they are in the plan. Older employees with fewer years until retirement prefer a defined benefit plan which can set benefits at the maximum allowed by law.

Unlike a pension plan, a profit-sharing plan does not have fixed benefits. Contributions are made out of corporate profits and allocated to the employees participating in the plan according to a definite formula. The allocation must not discriminate in favor of stockholders, officers, and executives. At retirement or other payout date (upon disability, for example), the employee receives the amount allocated to his or her account plus the income and capital appreciation attributable to the allocated amount. A profit-sharing plan is a type of defined contribution plan. The contribution is limited by a written formula; retirement benefits will be the amount that the accumulated contributions can buy upon retirement.

A pension plan should be considered only if the earnings record of your business shows a reasonable amount of stability. Pension plans call for regular contributions by your company, regardless of profits. A pension plan must be actuarially sound; the contributions must be sufficient to pay a fixed monthly sum to an employee who reaches retirement age and retires. To meet this obligation, the law imposes minimum standards; contributions are figured accordingly.

A profit-sharing plan is more flexible since your company is not obligated to pay a fixed annual amount into the fund. It may contribute according to a formula keyed to profits. In loss years it may contribute nothing, while in prosperous years contributions can be substantial. Profit-sharing plans furnish employee incentives to increase profits, whereas pension plans furnish the employee security through fixed and prearranged future benefits.

The selection of a particular plan depends on your projection of future business conditions. Other factors to be weighed are the rate of labor turnover, the ratio of young to older employees, and the tax burden. Pension plans favor older employees; profit-sharing plans favor younger employees.

Pension plans are more costly to administer. In addition to fees for actuarial computations, you are required to pay premiums to the Pension Benefit Guaranty Corporation on behalf of each employee covered by a pension plan. Premiums are designed to cover retirement benefits for plans that fail or are terminated before benefits are fully funded.

Pension plans and profit-sharing plans must provide for a trustee except in the case of an annuity pension plan in which contracts are bought from an insurance company. If you set up a pension plan and fund it by buying an annuity contract, you give up all control over the investment of plan funds. The insurance company handles the investments and guarantees payment of stipulated benefits.

If you use a trustee plan, your plan involves the creation of a trust which is responsible for the investment and payment of funds contributed to it. You may name yourself trustee and you will be subject to fiduciary responsibility rules.

To obtain maximum benefits for yourself, you must provide adequate benefits for your employees. Plans which are considered "top heavy" because they favor owners and key executives must provide set benefits to rank and file employees to maintain qualified status.

ADVANTAGES OF SALARY-REDUCTION PLANS

If your company gives you the opportunity to enter a cash or salary-reduction plan, you may benefit from tax savings and other advantages.

The cash or deferred-pay plan operates in one of two ways: (1) Your employer contributes an amount for your benefit to a trust account. You are not taxed on your employer's contribution. (2) You agree to take a salary reduction or to forgo a salary increase. An amount equal to the pay reduction is placed in a trust account for your benefit. The reduction is treated as your employer's contribution.

Income earned on the trust account accumulates tax free until it is withdrawn. At withdrawal, tax on the proceeds may be computed by using the ten-year averaging method which gives a considerable tax savings over the regular method of tax computation. You may not withdraw funds until you reach age 59½, retire, are separated from service (resign or have been discharged), became disabled, or show financial hardship.

Should you take a salary reduction? Taking a pay reduction may be an ideal way to defer income, benefit from a tax-free buildup of income, and take advantage of ten-year averaging at distribution.

EXAMPLE—

You earn $30,000 and agree to defer 10% of your pay by taking a salary reduction. $3000 is put into trust; your taxable pay reported on your Form W-2 for the year is $27,000 which you report on your tax return. Income earned on the $3000 is not taxed. When you withdraw your total account you can pay tax on the distribution using ten-year averaging.

Participating in a deferred-pay or salary-reduction plan does not prevent you from also contributing to an IRA account.

However, if your investment dollars are limited and you must choose between setting up your own IRA or contributing to a salary-reduction plan, consider the relative merits of each plan.

With an IRA, you must take the initiative to seek out an investment, such as a bank CD or an annuity. Further, you must meet your contribution obligation yourself. With a salary-reduction plan, you need only consent to the plan which is set up and administered by your company plan's trustees. Contributions are automatic; they are withheld from your pay and transferred to the plan.

You can take advantage of ten-year averaging. Ten-year averaging does not apply to IRA distributions.

APPLY FOR AN EXTENSION IF YOU CANNOT MEET THE FILING DEADLINE

If you need extra time to prepare your return, you may avoid certain penalties and automatically get an extra four months to do so by filing Form 4868, provided you also pay the full amount of your estimated tax bill.

As April 15 approaches and you find that you need more time to prepare your tax return, you may obtain an automatic four-month extension by filing Form 4868 by the regular due date. This will give you until August 15 instead of April 15 to file your return and will avoid the penalty for failure to file a timely return. Such a penalty is 5% of the amount of tax due for each month of delinquency up to a maximum of 25%. This extension does not apply to payment of your tax; it applies only to filing. In order to obtain the filing extension, you must pay the full amount you expect to owe and file Form 4868. If your estimate of the tax due is too low, you may be subject to a penalty. If you do not pay at least 90% of the actual tax bill when you file Form 4868, the IRS may assess a penalty equal to 0.5% of the unpaid tax for each month (or part of month) it is late, up to a maximum 25% penalty. You will also owe interest on any amount due after the regular filing date, despite the extension for filing.

What if your problem is not filing your return but paying your tax? You should file your return by April 15 and at the same time apply on Form 1127 for an extension of time to pay your tax. The IRS allows a payment extension only in cases of extreme financial hardship. You must demonstrate that you do not have assets with which to pay your tax and that you are unable to borrow the necessary amount. If you would have to sell property at a sacrifice price in order to raise the funds, the IRS will consider this hardship. If you meet the hardship test, a payment extension of up to six months may be allowed. You will still owe interest on the tax delayed after the regular due date.

100

AVOID ESTIMATED TAX PENALTY

You can avoid the high penalty for underestimating tax by using one of two common methods, described below.

A penalty is charged on the amount of underpayment of any installment of estimated tax. A reasonable excuse or lack of funds to pay does not bar the penalty.

You have made an underpayment if the total of your estimated tax payments plus withholdings from your salary is less than 80% (66⅔% for farmers and fishermen) of the tax shown on your final return.

The penalty is figured for each installment date. It runs until the amount is paid or until the filing rate for the final tax return, whichever is earlier. The penalty rate on an installment is applied to the difference between 20% of your final tax and estimated tax payments, if any, made for the quarter.

The most common and safest ways to avoid the penalty are:

1. In figuring your 1985 estimated tax, fix your tax at an amount equal to or more than the final tax shown on your 1984 return. This includes the self-employment tax, if any. To use this method, your 1984 return must cover a period of 12 months and show a tax liability.

EXAMPLE—

Your 1984 tax is $3,000. By fixing your 1985 estimated tax at $3,000 or more, you are not subject to penalties even if $3,000 is less than 80% of your 1985 tax. If you use this method, make sure you pay your quarterly payments on time. If you miss a quarterly payment and you have underestimated, you will be penalized for missing the quarter even if your later payments equal the 1984 tax.

2. You may avoid the penalty on an estimated tax installment based on income which was earned in the months ending before the due date of the installment and which was annualized for purposes of computing the estimated tax. At the time this book went to press, proposed regulations for applying this exception had not been released (*see* Form 2210).

3. You may avoid the penalty if you have no tax liability in the preceding taxable year which included 12 months. For example, if in 1984 you had no tax liability, you are not subject to estimated tax penalty for not paying a 1985 estimated tax. This exception applies only to U.S. citizens or a resident for the entire preceding taxable year.

Waiver of penalty for hardship, retirement or disability. The IRS may waive the penalty if you can show you failed to pay the estimated tax because of casualty, disaster, or other unusual circumstances. You may also avoid the penalty if you are 62 or over and retired in 1984 or 1985 and you failed to make a payment due to reasonable cause and not due to willful neglect. The same rule applies if you became disabled in 1984 or 1985.

101

GET THE MOST FROM A REFUND CLAIM

A refund may be denied because of your failure to comply with a technical rule. Protect your refund claim by filing on time and stating all the reasons for your claim.

Before you decide to file a tax refund claim, carefully review the return for accuracy. A refund claim opens the return to a thorough investigation; the IRS may find errors that reduce or completely eliminate the refund claim and may even lead to the assessment of a deficiency.

Some tax practitioners advise waiting until the end of the limitations period to file refund claims. If the IRS, after the limitations period, finds a deficiency, it can use the deficiency only to offset the claimed refund.

A refund claim for income taxes must be made within a set time limit and may not exceed a dollar limitation. The claim must be made within three years from the time the return was filed or two years from the time the tax was paid, whichever is later. For purposes of determining the three-year period, a return which is filed before the original due date (for example, on March 1) is deemed to have been filed on the due date (April 15). However, if an extension for filing is obtained, a return filed before the extended due date is deemed to have been filed on the actual date of filing and not on the extended due date.

You may file a protective refund claim when a particular issue is being litigated by other taxpayers and you want to await the outcome. This type of claim is generally accompanied by a cover letter to the IRS explaining its nature. Filing the protective refund claim preserves your right to sue for a refund. The period is two years from the mailing date of the district director's notice of disallowance of your claim.

The amount of the refund is limited to the amount of tax paid within the three-year period (plus any extensions of time for filing) preceding the filing of the claim, or if the claim is not filed within the three-year period, to the amount of tax paid within the two-year period preceding the filing of the claim.

Refund claims must be filed on Form 1040X (for an individual who originally filed on Form 1040 or 1040A) or on Form 1120X (for a corporation which filed Form 1120). If a form other than Form 1040, 1040A, or 1120 was filed, a refund claim is made on an amended return. Form 843 may be used for claiming a refund for employment taxes or certain other non-income taxes. You need not file a formal claim for overpayment of personal income tax resulting from excessive withholding of taxes on wages or excessive estimated tax payments. In these two cases a tax return requesting a refund of the overpayment acts as a claim for refund. There is one exception: on the death of an individual who has overpaid his tax, the administrator or executor of his estate files a refund claim on Form 1310.

The most important part of a refund claim is stating the reasons for the refund. A general claim simply noting an overpayment without supporting facts and grounds is not sufficient. If a claim is denied by the IRS, it may become the basis of a court suit. If you have not stated all the grounds, you may not be allowed to show them in court. The courts have limited taxpayers to the exact claim shown on the form. You must make a full claim. You have to show:

1. All the facts that support the claim. You may attach to the form as much evidence as is helpful. The language you use is not important. Just be sure your facts are simply and fully stated. If you need more space than the form provides, the statement and supporting exhibits must be on letter-size sheets ($8\frac{1}{2}'' \times 11''$).

2. All the grounds for the claim. You may hedge if you are uncertain about the exact grounds; alternate and even inconsistent grounds may be given. For example, the loss was incurred from an embezzlement; if not, from a bad debt. The gain from the sale is entitled to capital gain treatment since the property sold was a capital asset; if not, it was depreciable property used in business.

While it is necessary to be complete and precise in specifying the facts and reasons for your claim, you are not required to present your evidence. You must merely inform the IRS of the basis for your claim.

To protect against understating the amount of your claim, it may be advisable to preface the claim with this phrase: "The following or such greater amounts as may be legally refunded." However, neither this nor any other "protective clause" will allow you to support your refund claim on grounds other than those mentioned in the original claim or in amendments made before the period of limitations has expired.

A separate claim must be made for each year a refund is claimed.